Standards Battles in Open Source Software

Standards Battles in Open Source Software

The Case of Firefox

Huibert de Vries

Henk de Vries

and

Ilan Oshri

First published 2008 by
PALGRAVE MACMILLAN

Palgrave Macmillan in the UK is an imprint of Macmillan Publishers Limited, registered in England, company number 785998, of Houndmills, Basingstoke, Hampshire RG21 6XS.

Palgrave Macmillan in the US is a division of St Martin's Press LLC, 175 Fifth Avenue, New York, NY 10010.

Palgrave Macmillan is the global academic imprint of the above companies and has companies and representatives throughout the world.

Palgrave® and Macmillan® are registered trademarks in the United States, the United Kingdom, Europe and other countries.

ISBN-13: 978-0-230-22072-0 hardback
ISBN-10: 0-230-22072-X hardback

This book is printed on paper suitable for recycling and made from fully managed and sustained forest sources. Logging, pulping and manufacturing processes are expected to conform to the environmental regulations of the country of origin.

A catalogue record for this book is available from the British Library.

Library of Congress Cataloging-in-Publication Data

Vries, Huibert de.
    Standards battles in open source software : the case of Firefox / Huibert de Vries, Henk de Vries, and Ilan Oshri.
        p. cm.
    ISBN 978-0-230-22072-0 (alk. paper)
    1. Open source software – Standards. 2. Browsers (Computer programs) 3. Firefox. I. Vries, Henk J. de. II. Oshri, Ilan. III. Title.

QA76.76.S46V75 2008
005.7'1376—dc22   2008029951

10 9 8 7 6 5 4 3 2 1
17 16 15 14 13 12 11 10 09 08

Printed and bound in Great Britain by
CPI Antony Rowe, Chippenham and Eastbourne

The fear of the LORD is the beginning of knowledge

Proverbs 1:7a

Contents

List of Figures

List of Tables

Preface

The browser war between Firefox and Internet Explorer presents an intriguing case: how did Firefox manage to achieve a relatively significant market share in a 'winner-takes-all' industry? Why did Firefox manage to gain some market share while other competitors have failed? Is this because of the Open Source characteristics of the Firefox browser? These questions were the starting point of our research into standard-setting mechanisms in OSS. The battle for dominance in the browser industry was the case through which we sought to explore the influence of Open Source Software on standards-setting in the software industry. This turned out to be an interesting exercise, and we are happy to be able to share our findings through this book.

We would like to thank Najim Argam for contributing to the updates made in this manuscript in late 2007.

We wish the readers of this book the same fascinating and insightful encounter with the world of browser wars, standards-setting and open source software as we experienced while conducting this research and writing this story!

HUIBERT DE VRIES, HENK DE VRIES, ILAN OSHRI
Rotterdam, April 25, 2008

Acknowledgments

Huibert would like to give special thanks to his parents and sisters for their continuous encouragement and support. I am very grateful for the bond we share, for better and worse. They also rightfully remind me that there is more to life than knowledge and success alone.

I also owe a lot to my professors at Rotterdam School of Management, Erasmus University and Brandeis University's International Business School. They not only instilled academic rigor, but, with their enthusiasm and the thought-provoking way they conducted their classes, challenged me to strive for excellence, be curious and go that 'extra mile'. Looking back, I can only conclude that my studies at these reputable institutes, and the extra-curricular activities I was able to do, were a crucial learning period.

Many thanks go also to my friends and my colleagues at Philips. I'm privileged to have people like them around.

Particular thanks go to my co-authors, Henk de Vries and Ilan Oshri. The dedication and the insights they brought to the table not the least explains the success of this project. On top of that, it was a pleasure to collaborate in the way that we did.

Henk would like to thank Huibert and Ilan for the cooperation which enabled this result: the trajectory was a real pleasure. We started our research on standards battles and open source software without the intention and expectation that this would result in a book. Ilan, I hope this common achievement can form the starting point for future cooperation in other projects: I enjoyed your approach. Huibert and Najim: the cooperation with you was a real personal experience which I appreciated very much.

I also have to thank my family. The many possibilities the Rotterdam School of Management offers have to be balanced with family life and in this case I used the main part of the Christmas holiday for the book...I thank you all very much for your love and understanding.

Ilan would also like to thank his colleagues at Rotterdam School of Management. The RSM has been a good place for me: it is a challenging research institution and at times also very competitive, which keeps the faculty on their toes. I wish to thank Henk de Vries and Huibert de Vries for sharing their knowledge with me about open source software and standards battles. These past three years of working with you, Henk and Huibert, have been an excellent learning experience.

Last but not least, Ilan would like to thank his wife, Julia Kotlarsky, for all her love, support, and stimulus to live life to the utmost. Every single moment with you Julia is a joy.

The authors are indebted to Najim Argam who joined our team at a later stage and provided case updates and a more coherent set of references. We also thank Mr. Nigel Prentice for the thorough proofreading of our book. The authors would also like to thank the team of Palgrave MacMillan for their interest in our project and for the hard work through each step on the way to making this project a book!

1
Introduction

The battle for the dominant standard in the web browser industry is a fascinating example of a standards competition. Several studies (Bresnahan and Yin, 2007; Sebenius, 2002; Yoffie and Cusumano, 1999) have been dedicated to the Internet browser war between Microsoft Internet Explorer (IE) versus Netscape (Communicator) in the 1990s, leaving Microsoft's IE as the standard web browser. In 2002, IE controlled an estimated 95% of the browser market (Onestat. com, 2002[1]), a seemingly impregnable position.

However, a new struggle in the web browser industry has emerged: surprisingly, Mozilla's open source web browser Firefox has started to make inroads into the market at a rapid pace since 2004, at IE's expense. By September 2007, IE's market share had decreased to 74%, Firefox had a 21% market share, and the other browsers together 4% (XiTi, 2007[2]). Other sources provide different figures but the tendency is clear: Firefox has been squeezing IE's market share to an increasing extent.

This turn of events contradicts current wisdom: in an industry with network effects such as the web browser industry, the strong, in this case, IE, should grow stronger (Shapiro and Varian, 1999a, b), and not weaker. In general, models of the diffusion of technological innovations under conditions of increasing returns to adoption, and which are built on path dependence and lock-in (Arthur, 1989; David, 1985), predict that in the long term a single dominant technology will prevail, which, once established, prevents competing technologies from obtaining a foothold in the market (Bonaccorsi et al., 2004).

Although the browser wars have similarities – in both cases a late entrant takes on an established incumbent – there are also profound differences. The first browser war took place in a "pre-*open source software* (OSS)" setting (Netscape vs Microsoft), while in the second (Microsoft vs Mozilla) the proprietary incumbent is subject to competition from an OSS rival. Therefore the question arises as to whether Firefox's rise in market share and current coexistence with IE are related to the fact that it is OSS, and whether OSS does influence the manner in which a standard becomes dominant. Standards-setting and competition in the web browser industry in general have received much attention. Most of the studies concern the browser war between IE and Netscape Communicator (e.g., Corts and Freier, 2003; Cusumano and Yoffie, 1998; Jenkins et al., 2004; Windrum, 2004). Except for the study by Wang, Wu and Lin (2005), none of the studies on competition and standards-setting in the browser industry so far take into account the new situation of the OSS browser Firefox gaining market share over IE, although there are studies that touch upon this development of Firefox (Krishnamurthy, 2005a; Mockus et al., 2002) and Firefox's marketing campaign (Krishnamurthy, 2005b).

Most research on OSS to date has focused on the organization and management issues surrounding OSS (Silverthorne, 2005), for example, its development (Raymond, 1999; Spinellis and Szyperski, 2004), its development coordination (Crowston et al., 2005; Egyedi and Van Wendel de Joode, 2004) and the economic rationale of OSS contributors (Frost, 2005; Lerner and Tirole, 2000). Aside from studies on Linux (Casadesus-Masanell and Ghemawat, 2006), not much research has been conducted into the standards-setting and competition of OSS or into proprietary software in the marketplace.

The origins of OSS can be found in the sixties and seventies, but the rise of Linux has drawn it into the spotlight. Raymond (1998a) defines OSS as software for which the source code is publicly available and which permits changes by users. Frost (2005) refers to open source as two separate, yet related entities, the open source development model, and the open source style of licensing. OSS development can be characterized as a "bazaar" (Raymond, 1999), where software is cooperatively developed by voluntary contributions in an open and participatory environment. Or, as Frost (2005) puts it, OSS development is a process of developing software based on decentralization, collaboration, and reciprocity. OSS need not necessarily be completely developed from scratch by volunteers. Sometimes, established firms release proprietary code into open source. As Lerner and Tirole (2004) observe, this usually happens when a company is lagging behind the market leaders.

Besides its distinctive approach of development, open source licensing is another unique aspect of OSS. The three key tenets usually embodied in an open source license are: "free redistribution", "open source code", and "allowed derived works" (Fink, 2003). Although there is consensus that OSS users should be able to read, use and modify the source code, different views exist on the appropriability and on the blending of OSS with proprietary software (West and Dedrick, 2001). These different views have led to different OSS licenses, of which the Berkeley Software Distribution (BSD) license and the more restrictive GPL license, to be explained later, are the best known.

The alleged pros and cons of OSS have been the subject of a heated debate. Mendys-Kamphorst (2002) has identified the most common advantages of OSS, such as lower price, higher reliability, customization, no vendor lock-in, and availability of support, while the most common disadvantages include lack of agent responsibility, incompleteness and poor integration, low user-friendliness, absence of complements, and lack of compatibility between versions.

OSS's compatibility deserves special attention, as it has a strong relation to standards-setting. Compatibility is relevant both in the development phase of an OSS product and in the market context. It can be split up in terms of compatibility between different versions of the same product, which Katz and Shapiro (1994) term vertical compatibility, and in terms of compatibility with other products, which Katz and Shapiro (1994) term horizontal compatibility.

Once an OSS program is ready, its promotion can be sponsored, in the sense that Oshri and Weeber (2006: 4) define as sponsoring of the program: "a variety of activities aiming to promote the technology or product in order to establish it as a market standard." Three strategic options by which a firm or OSS sponsor can compete in the market have been identified by Hax and Wilde (1999): "Best Product", "System Lock-in", and "Total-customer Solutions".

Standard, in the context of this study, refers to a complete virtual product (i.e., the web browser). A standard achieves dominance in the case that its market share is over 50%.

Oshri and Weeber (2006) define three main standards-setting attributes they believe influence the manner a standard emerges: "effort to standardize", "mode of standard selection", and "access to standard", framed along the cooperation–competition continuum.

Standards can be distinguished between open and closed proprietary. A proprietary standard's access is owned and controlled by one party, whereas, in the case of an open standard, access to the standard is open to all (Grant, 2002). Standards are not easily classified into "open" or "closed", as they encompass varying degrees of openness. Openness can also be measured in different manners. West (2004) identifies three key metrics for openness, while Krechmer (2006) identifies ten different measures of openness. Shapiro and Varian (1999a, b) also address the rationale of an open standard and further elaborate on the consequences and trade-offs of standard openness.

Standardization mechanisms, the theoretical mechanisms that underlie standards' acceptance in the market, have received wide attention in the literature (Farrel and Saloner, 1985; Katz and Shapiro, 1985, 1992; Shapiro and Varian, 1999a, b). Classical concepts in this respect are network effects, positive feedback, and lock-in. Network effects refer to a situation where the value of a product for an individual user increases when the number of people who use the product increase (Grant, 2002). Positive feedback is the phenomenon of a self-reinforcing circle of success (Shapiro and Varian, 1999b). In the case of lock-in, users are not willing to abandon the standard they have adopted because the cost of switching to a new standard is too significant.

Different standards may compete for acceptance. Shapiro and Varian (1999a) have identified two tactics for participants that often occur in such standards wars: preemption and expectation management. They further identify seven key assets needed to win a standards war, for example, control over installed user base, and reputation and brand name (Shapiro and Varian, 1999a).

Book structure

This book is structured as follows. Chapters 2 and 3 provide overviews of the literature on OSS and standards-setting respectively. Chapter 4 offers a framework to examine standardization battles. We will use this frame when examining the Mozilla and Microsoft case. Chapter 5 provides a description of the industry, from the PC industry at large to the more specific web browser industry. The second part of this chapter introduces the web browser industry's main players, Microsoft and Mozilla, their history and certain issues relating to the context of the study. Chapter 6 describes Browser War I (IE vs Netscape), while Chapter 7 outlines Browser War II (Firefox vs IE). We examine these two standardization battles through the lens of our framework. We analyze the manner the standardization battles are carried out in OSS in Chapter 8 and draw conclusions concerning the impact that OSS has had on these battles. Finally, we discuss implications for practice and research in Chapter 9.

2
Open Source Software

Origin and evolution

The roots of "open source software" (OSS) go back to the practices of scientific research organizations of the 1960s and 1970s, such as Bell Labs, Xerox Park and the University of California at Berkeley, where this type of voluntary "code sharing" was quite common (Raymond, 1999).

The open source movement in its current form emerged because a number of skilled programmers, such as Richard Stallman and Linus Torvalds, were frustrated at not being able to improve commercial software due to the lack of an available source[1] code as well as its protection by patents, copyrights, and restrictive licenses. These programmers wanted to write better programs with codes that would be generally free and available to anyone in source-code format to improve upon, as long as such authors made the improvements available to everyone else (Cusumano, 2004).[2]

Two famous examples of OSS are Linux and Apache. Linux is an operating system of which the kernel was developed in 1991 by Linus Torvalds. This operating system was developed via the Internet, and is considered to be the only credible threat to complete Windows dominance (Kenwood, 2001). Apache is a much-used web server that hosts websites and databases. In recent years the success of several OSS programs, such as the Linux operating system and Apache server packages, has made them viable alternatives to several common software programs. Other examples of successful open source projects are Berkeley Software Distribution (BSD), Mozilla, MySQL and RPG Toolkit. Open source also includes scripting languages such as Perl, which are behind most "live" content on the Internet.

Fuggetta (2003) identifies three factors that explain the increased interest in OSS: (1) the success of software packages such as Linux and Apache; (2) the discomfort relating to the Microsoft monopoly in the software market; and (3) the perception that conventional approaches to software development fail to meet the demands for effective and trustworthy software.

One can also use the "supply/demand concept" to explain the continuing success of OSS. The increase in popularity can then be explained by noting that, on the supply side, the Internet has been a useful facilitator in coordinating open source projects around the globe. Demand has increased due to the already-mentioned advantages of OSS and the credibility that programs like Apache and Linux have brought to OSS.

The adoption of OSS packages seems more and more to be driven by non-profit-making institutions. In particular, European, Asian and South American governments and public institutions are buying in to OSS. The motives that lead governments to support it are: (1) that OSS is considered to be a viable alternative to the dominant US technology, and governments believe that by supporting OSS they also stimulate the software industry in their country or region; (2) that it makes them less dependent on one supplier; and (3) that they are concerned about the security issues surrounding most proprietary software (Fuggetta, 2003).

While the popularity of OSS is increasing, Cusumano (2004) doubts whether companies will ever make a profit by providing services surrounding OSS. In his view, the software sector will continue to see a blend of free, open source, and proprietary software products. This is also predicted by the World Bank's report on OSS (World Bank, 2005). The report sees the benefit of OSS in the fact that it increases choice in IT options: new solutions can be a mix of both proprietary and OSS. Microsoft have acknowledged the value of providing access to its source code and made it available as a "feature" of some products such as Windows CE under the "Shared Source Initiative," but some 95% of its users never actually choose to exercise this right (Fitzgerald et al., 2005). Bonaccorsi and Rossi (2003) argue that in many plausible situations commercial software and OSS are likely to coexist. Lerner and Tirole (2004), while acknowledging that improvements in the OSS are not appropriable, believe that commercial software firms can still make money by offering their expertise in a proprietary segment of the market complementary to the open source program. Wichmann (2002) has investigated the involvement in Open Source development activities of the world's 25 largest software companies. He has found that one-third of these firms engaged in major Open Source development activities while three companies had smaller projects.

The idiom "open source" was first coined by Raymond (1999). It was meant as a substitute for the term "free software" as espoused by the Free Software Foundation (FSF), and which was prone to duality in meaning. The FSF had intended the word to mean "free as in free speech," not "free as in free beer" (Williams, 2002). Free software also had a dubious ring to most businessmen, who believed that they couldn't make money from software that was for free.

It was hoped that the use of the newer term "open source" would eliminate such ambiguity, particularly for users who might mistakenly associate "free software" with anti-commercialism. The phrase has, however, become the focus of a modest terminology battle among open source and free software advocates ever since (Stallman, 1998; Perens, 1999). "Open source" in essence incorporates the same licensing practices as those established by the "free software" movement. It differs from the "free software" movement primarily on philosophical grounds, emphasizing the practical benefits of its licensing practices over issues regarding the moral rightness of granting users the freedom offered by both free and open source software (von Krogh and von Hippel, 2003). Nowadays, the expression "open source" or OSS is generally used to refer to both free and open source labeled software. In common usage the term "open source" refers to any software with a publicly available source code. "Open source" describes two separate yet related entities (Frost, 2005), which make it uniquely distinct from proprietary software. The first of these is the open source *development* model, which is a manner of developing software based on decentralization, collaboration and reciprocity and also allows for changes by users after the initial development of the program. The other main entity that is often referred to by the term "open source" is the open source style of software *licensing*, which deals with issues of access and control and which allows for access to the source code. The interpretation of OSS adopted in this study thus comprises these two elements: an open development model, and a publicly available source code which permits changes by users. The next section deals with the development aspects of OSS in more detail.

OSS development

Eric Raymond's seminal essay "The Cathedral and the Bazaar" (Raymond, 1999) can be regarded as the manifesto of the open source movement. Raymond compares two different free software development models: The "cathedral" symbolizes a development model in which the source code is freely available with each software release. Between the releases the code is developed by an exclusive group of developers. This process resembles the manner Europeans built cathedrals in the Middle Ages. In contrast, the "bazaar" exemplifies a model in which software is developed for public purposes as in the case of Linux.

Over time the "cathedral" concept has also been used to describe the common top-down, hierarchical software design philosophies that typify how proprietary software is developed, although there has been criticism that this analogy has become outdated with new development processes in proprietary software development, whereas the term "bazaar" is used to describe the participative manner in which open source software is developed.

Raymond's proposition is that "Given enough eyeballs, all bugs are shallow" (Raymond, 1999). His essay argues that, if the source code is available for public testing and experimentation, bugs will be discovered at a rapid rate. "The Cathedral and the Bazaar" received wide acceptance in the free software community and eventually inspired Netscape to release the source of Netscape Communicator.

In short, therefore, OSS development distinguishes itself in that software is cooperatively developed mostly from scratch by voluntary contributions from developers all over the world in an open and participatory environment. OSS projects have their own development sites on the Internet to which the contributions can be submitted and through which they can be evaluated. Contributions are typically examined by a small group of project leaders,[3] who decide on the inclusion or non-inclusion of the code in the program (Mendys-Kamphorst, 2002). The distinct manner in which OSS has developed and the fact that it allows for adaptation after the release of a product is expected to be of influence on the standards-setting, as will be clarified below. OSS is not always developed from scratch. Sometimes established software companies also release existing proprietary code, usually accompanied by a newly created license that governs the terms of use. HP, for instance, released code to help the Linux community write software to connect Linux with HP's reduced instruction set computing (RISC) computer architecture, and IBM released Eclipse, a suite of developers' tools. The underlying rationale for releasing the code is generally to give the razor in order to sell more razor blades. This is similar to the idea of giving away the source code in order to benefit from consulting services or to stimulate the sales of complementary proprietary products. In general, source code release should only be considered when profits in complementary proprietary segments offset the profits that are foregone by the release of the source code.

Microsoft joined the crowd in 2001 by setting up a "Shared Source Initiative"[4], to address security concerns and to help developers optimize integration with Microsoft products (Nuttall, 2005). This initiative offers different Shared Source License Programs to Microsoft customers, partners and governments.[5] Licensees can access the source codes of various programs, depending on their license. Only major customers and governments obtain access to the most secret parts of the source code. However, unlike most open source licenses, the authors maintain strict control over the use of that code once it has been read, and modification of the source code is not allowed.[6]

Lerner and Tirole (2004) observe that commercial companies usually release source code when the company is lagging behind the market leaders. By releasing part of the source code, the company hopes to increase adoption of its product, enhancing its chances to set a technological standard.

OSS licenses

The license an OSS program is governed by represents the second unique aspect of OSS, next to its distinctive development. To clarify what makes a software license "open-source", the Open Source Initiative (OSI) has created a framework known as the Open Source Definition (OSD) of about ten key licensing terms that, if employed in a license, will designate the licensed code as "open source" (Fink, 2003; Coar, 2006). Three key tenets are embodied in these terms:

Free redistribution: The recipient of the program can give it away to anybody.

Open source code: The program must expose its source code in a readable and modifiable format.

Allowed derived works: The recipient must have the ability to make and distribute a derivative program from the licensed code and be able to use the same licensing terms.

Although there is consensus in the open source community that OSS users should be able to read, use and modify their source code, different views exist on appropriability and on the blending of OSS with proprietary software (West and Dedrick, 2001).[7]

An overview of the different software licenses can be found in Table 2.1. Subsequently each license is concisely described.[8]

OS – BSD-license: BSD-based open source projects typically resemble the software development organization of a proprietary firm where development is undertaken and carefully coordinated by a small group of people (West and Dedrick, 2001). The "public" therefore

Table 2.1 Overview of software licenses

Software license		License features					
	Zero price	Redistri-butable	Unlimited usage	Source Code available	Source Code modifiable	OSS can be mixed with non-OSS	All deriva-tives must be free[a]
Commercial software							
Trial software	X	X					
Freeware	X	X	X				
Royalty-free libraries	X	X	X	X			
OS – BSD license	X	X	X	X	X	X	
OS – Mozilla public license	X	X	X	X	X	X	
OS –GPL license	X	X	X	X	X		X

Notes: [a] That is, proprietary distribution is allowed.

Source: West and Dedrick, 2001; Perens, 1999 and Halloween Documents, 1998 http://opensource.feratech.com/halloween/halloween1.php, last accessed on December 8, 2007.

cannot make changes to the "core code". The BSD license was originally used for the Unix distributions released by the University of California at Berkeley. The BSD license allows for freely copying and modifying the source code but is less restrictive than the General Public License (GPL) because it allows maximum freedom in using the source code to create derivative works. This includes the freedom to take open-source software under a BSD-style license and use it to create a proprietary, commercial derivative for which the source code is not made available (Hecker, 2000).

OS – Mozilla Public License[9] (MPL): MPL and the related Netscape Public License[10] were created by Netscape as part of the project to release Netscape Communicator's source code. The MPL and variants go further than the BSD and similar licenses in discouraging "software hoarding"[11] but still allow developers to create proprietary add-ons if they wish (Hecker, 2000). The MPL stipulates that source code copied or changed under the MPL must stay under the MPL. However, code may be combined in a program with proprietary files. Thus, a proprietary version of an "MPLed" open source program may be released (http://www.mozilla.org/MPL/MPL-1.1.html, 2005). For example, Netscape 6 and 7 are proprietary versions of corresponding releases of the Mozilla Suite. Like the BSD, proprietary software compiled with OSS does not need to become OSS as well, as long as the original source code is acknowledged. Microsoft, for instance, has used source code from the BSD operating system in its Windows 2000 and XP products (Krishnamurthy, 2003).

OS – GPL: GPL-oriented open source projects are largely without structure and accept contributions from anyone; based on the feedback of thousands of users, it decides which changes are accepted and which are rejected (West and Dedrick, 2001). Linux is the most famous example. The GPL is in many ways the opposite of the BSD license, and the most restrictive of all open source licenses. Where BSD-style licenses essentially permit unlimited commercial use of open source software and in effect unrestricted creation of proprietary derivative works, the GPL is intentionally designed to prevent open source software from being used to create proprietary derivative works. GPL stipulates that all enhancements to the source code – even if they are blended together with proprietary software – become licensed under the GPL as well (making the proprietary software OSS too). Derivatives of a program licensed under the GPL must also be licensed under the GPL. The license also requires that programs licensed under the GPL must be distributed without a license fee (which essentially means that all derivative works have to be free) and with the source code made available.

Open source software is sometimes confused with "public domain" software. This kind of software is not copyrighted, and in contrast to OSS there are no restrictions on its modification and distribution.

Advantages and disadvantages

OSS has certain distinctive features and characteristics but, according to Fuggetta (2003), most of these associated with OSS development also apply to proprietary software and it is not proven that OSS is better, more reliable or cheaper to develop. Mendys (2002), however, identifies several advantages and disadvantages of OSS as mentioned by users and developers that follow from its unique process of development and licensing, distinctive from proprietary software. These advantages include:

Lower price: The source code is available for free, and OSS can be downloaded free of charge from websites or bought for a minor fee on CD-ROM.

Higher reliability: Anybody can inspect the source code and provide solutions for possible bugs. Therefore, OSS is more reliable than proprietary software.

Customization: OSS allows end-users to customize the programs to their specific needs, either by themselves or through a specialized commercial firm.

No vendor lock-in: Users are not dependent on a specific supplier for technical support, because anybody with the appropriate knowledge can make changes to the source code.

Availability of support: Even after the original creator has abandoned the project, support can still be provided. The open nature of the software ensures that there always is someone who knows the ins and outs of the program.

The disadvantages are also multiple, and the most commonly mentioned are:

Lack of agent responsibility for development, quality or support: Commercial software firms are legally responsible for their product, which stimulates them to maintain at least a minimum level of quality.

Incompleteness and poor integration: Because OSS development is mostly voluntary, the less attractive elements of programming are sometimes simply skipped. The OSS development approach of splitting the project into mostly independently developed modules may lead to poor integration at the overall level.

Low user-friendliness: OSS presupposes a certain amount of knowledge, which makes the software too difficult for many less skilled users.

Absence of complements: Complementary software, for example applications for OSS operating systems, is often not available.

Lack of compatibility between versions: Due to the decentralized manner in which OSS is developed it may run the risk that many more or less incompatible versions emerge. This may be due to "forking," when during the development different views on how to continue lead to the split-up into separate and independently developed projects. Incompatibility may also arise as a result of adaptations at the user level.

Compatibility

Compatibility issues related to software programs deserve special attention when dealing with standards-setting. This applies to proprietary software as well as to open source software. As will be explained later on, the compatibility of a product may be of great influence in attracting enough users to succeed in the market. Katz and Shapiro (1998: 4) define compatibility as follows: "When two programs can communicate with one another and/or be used with the same complementary system components, they are said to be compatible."

Compatibility between different versions of the same product

Generally, more advanced versions of a product are introduced to the market over time. The presence of different versions adds to the compatibility complexity by adding the dimension of compatibility between different versions of the same product. Katz and Shapiro (1994) term this "vertical compatibility". This type of compatibility can be divided in turn into backward and forward compatibility (Simons and De Vries, 2002).

A system is backwards compatible if it is compatible with earlier versions of itself, or sometimes other earlier systems, particularly systems it intends to supplant. That is, other systems or objects that interoperate with the old version of the system should continue to do so with the new version. For instance, MS Word 2003 can read MS Word 2000 files.

Forward compatibility relates to the ability of a system to accept input from later versions of itself. For instance, when Philips and Sony specified the compact disc in 1982, the Philips delegates already knew that the CD-ROM should be backwards compatible with the CD. Therefore, the CD was made forward compatible with the CD-ROM (Simons and De Vries, 2002). Forward compatibility is harder to achieve than backward compatibility, since, in the case of backward compatibility, the input format is known, whereas a program that aims to be forward compatible needs to anticipate unknown future program features. As mentioned above, compatibility between different versions of the same software product is more challenging in the OSS case than in case of proprietary software.

Compatibility with other products

Shapiro and Varian (1999b) identified four product compatibility options on the compatible–incompatible spectrum, which represent the different compatibility possibilities between rival products, termed "horizontal compatibility," by Katz and Shapiro (1994). Meng and Lee (2005) identified four different compatibility options[12] in approaching OSS from a proprietary software viewpoint: incompatibility, two-manner compatibility, inward compatibility, and outward compatibility (Meng and Lee, 2005):

1. *Incompatibility*: a proprietary software product is not compatible with the OSS product (e.g., MS Windows is incompatible with Linux).
2. *Two-manner compatibility*: a proprietary software product is compatible with an open source product, and vice versa.

3. *Inward compatibility*: A proprietary software product is compatible with an OSS product, but not the other way around. For example, the web server Microsoft IIS is compatible with Apache, but Apache does not support files created by Microsoft IIS.

4. *Outward compatibility*: Files or programs designed for the proprietary software program can also be used by the OSS program, while files or programs designed for the open source software are not usable by the proprietary software program. However, this seldom occurs.

Creating compatibility with proprietary software may be hindered by lack of availability of the source code.

Promotion

Once an OSS program is ready for its first release to the general public, the product can be promoted through three basic forms. The organization or entity driving the development and promotion of the software is termed the "sponsor."

The first, and most common, form is promotion sponsorship by a commercial firm, like Red Hat with Linux. The mere existence of these OSS-oriented commercial firms suggests that at least several OSS products offer viable business opportunities, therefore challenging the idea that without Intellectual Property Rights (IPR) there are few or no economic returns. OSS proponents strongly believe in the business potential of "open source," whose foundation rests on OSS's reliability and quality. The open source community puts forward four "business models" for OSS:

1. *Service Seller*: The firm offers OSS distribution[13], branding and after-sale service for a charge. For example, Red Hat, which offers manuals, supporting applications, and so on.

2. *Loss Leader/Market Positioner*: The firm gives away previously proprietary OSS in order to attract future complementary business related to the OSS or to ensure a viable market position as Netscape aimed to do with Mozilla that will enable it to reap benefits in related market segments.

3. *Widget frosting*: A hardware company, for example, a semiconductor manufacturer, opens up its source code. This is typically

the case for hardware companies for whom software is a cost rather than a profit. By shifting to open source, these firms aim to obtain expensive drivers and interface tools free of any charge.
4. *Accessorizing*: Selling OSS-related accessories, for example, books and compatible hardware.

Krishnamurthy (2003) compares two types of models: one where the company sells OSS and provides service, and one in which a company only offers support. He notes that the company that only sells OSS must be able to add considerable value to the product in order to generate sufficient revenue. A company that only sells OSS can add value by selecting the best version given the customer needs, or by providing a suite of well-integrated products. Krishnamurthy concludes that the sale of software alone is generally insufficient to sustain the business. Companies are advised to engage in providing services as well.

Given that the focus of this study is on the software side, only the first two options, "Service Seller" and "Market Positioner," are relevant. Both options are essentially derived from the classical "razor and blades" business model: offer OSS for free, in order to charge money for related products or services. The main value proposition of OSS thus lies not in the "product" itself, which is offered for free, but in the related services.

The second basic option is promotion sponsorship by a platform. This can refer to a consortium of cooperating firms, for example Eclipse, which includes IBM, HP, Oracle, SAP and Red Hat, or a non-profit organization or platform sponsored by the OSS community that has a facilitating role in the spread of the OSS.

Finally, there can be a situation in which no direct sponsor exists at all. The programs can be downloaded from a general website listing OSS projects[14], and can be considered as sponsored by the OSS community at large. This is the fate of most OSS programs which are either inferior, less relevant or not yet discovered by the general public.

Depending on the sponsor's intentions, the resources it possesses, and the environmental constraints it faces, the sponsor is expected to engage in promotion and competitive activities in the acceptance phase in order to spread the software, in the hope that it will establish a dominant position in the market.

The Delta Model

From a strategic management viewpoint, there are three strategic options by which a firm or sponsor can compete in the market (Hax and Wilde, 1999). The concept, also known as the Delta Model, presented by Hax and Wilde was developed because *ex ante* theories on competition fall short when trying to explain the incredible success of companies like Microsoft. Most of these theories outline, in accordance with Porter, two basic ways to compete: on differentiation and on price. However, the products of companies like Microsoft are neither the best in their category nor the lowest in price. Hax and Wilde believed, therefore, that the new business environment and complexity of the "networked economy" warranted an extension of the current theories on competition that we hope to apply and extend in this work. In this regard, the Delta Model identifies three potential strategic options for competition: Best Product, Total Customer Solutions, and System Lock-in (Hax and Wilde, 1999: 12, Hax, 2002).[15] These options, which are not *per se* mutually exclusive, can be framed in a triangle on which also the position of firms can be indicated.

The "Best Product" strategic option refers to the traditional way to compete, through either low cost or differentiation. The "Total Customer Solutions" option relates to a strategy that focuses on customer economics rather than on product economics, for example, by offering a wide range of products and services that satisfies customers' needs. Finally, the "System Lock-in" option espouses a competition based on system economics, considering all the meaningful players in the system that contribute to the creation of value. Companies that hold the de facto standards in their industry are in the "System Lock-in" position. The "System Lock-in" option pays much attention to the role of complementors.

The notion of competition in terms of "system lock-in" seems particularly applicable to one of the cases under study, namely, IE in Browser War I, and to network industries in general. The model has credentials in explaining the success of Microsoft and other companies in the network industry, and highlights the phases by which a product can become a proprietary standard. Furthermore, companies create a proprietary standard through a "bonding continuum". Bonding deals with linking the product or service with the customer, in which a proprietary standard is the most extreme bonding mechanism (Hax and Wilde, 1999). The bonding continuum is made up of four stages: (1) Attract customers and establish as a first mover a dominant design; (2) lock in customers by creating switching costs; (3) lock out competitors; and (4) achieve and sustain a proprietary standard by ensuring the availability of complementary products. How such competitive dynamics play a role in the OSS industry still remains to be explored.

3
Standards and Standards-Setting

The concept of a standard

The term "standard" lends itself to multiple usages in different fields. Based on a review of *ex ante* literature, Grindley (1992) identified three types of standards: (1) minimum attributes that cover basic product requirements and minimum quality, for example, ISO 9000 standards or safety standards; (2) interface requirements that enable interoperability when products are connected, for example, the HTTP standard that enables web browsers to communicate with web servers; and (3) standards in the sense of standard product characteristics: features that define a group of similar products, for example, the WinTel P.C. The contribution of Grindley is only one of many standard categorizations. More can be found in De Vries (1998).

The standards concerned in this study fall into the second category of Grindley's classification, the compatibility standards. In line with this we will use the definition developed by Van der Kaa (2005: 4)[1]: a standard is *a codified specification defining the interrelations between entities, in order to enable them to function together.*

Standards for software; software as a standard

A well-known standard for mobile telecommunication is GSM. In fact, however, GSM has been made up from a range of technical standards (Bekkers, 2001; ETSI, 2007). So the concept of "standard" can be applied at two levels: a technology as a whole and its constituent technical standards. This may apply to software products as well: standards may be used to specify parts of the software, for example, a standard programming language or the international standard ISO 8601 which specifies the format of dates and times (ISO, 2004), or the entire software specification may be concerned. In both cases, the term "standard" refers to the specifications of the product/technology, specifications that are intended and expected to be used repeatedly or continuously by a substantial number of the parties for whom they are intended (De Vries, 1997). Because software is a "virtual product," the product and its specifications are almost the same, but there remains a slight difference (De Vries, 1998). The manufacturer of the software may have the intention and the expectation that these specifications will become widely accepted in the market, and in this sense it can be regarded as a standard. Standardization, in this case, is not the professional process of creating software, but it is the determination and recording of the software specifications (De Vries, 1998). Krechmer (2002) uses the example of a specific software program which is used as a test-bed for testing: then, the specific program in the test-bed takes on the characteristics of a technical standard. He also adds the example of a technical standard represented in the form of an Abstract Symbol Notation (ASN), being a formal logical language defining a communications protocol – this may be compiled into an operational software program. In the particular case of open source software (OSS), there may be continuous improvements of the software, and then it cannot be regarded as a standard because the stability which is essential for a standard is lacking (Krechmer, 2002).

The notion of an *(OSS) software as (open) standard* thus seems appropriate in the context of this study, but only in the case that there is a form of stability, for instance in the form of subsequent versions of the software that remain stable during a certain period of time.

Standards and dominant designs

When a software program, for example, Word, gains a significant market share, it can be considered as a dominant design. The concepts of standard and dominant design are sometimes used interchangeably, but Gallagher (2007) argues that they are fundamentally different. Gallagher quotes Shapiro and Varian (1999b: 228) in defining standard as "an interface format that creates a single network of compatible users" (Shapiro and Varian, 1999b: 372). By comparing this definition with the above ones, we can see that Shapiro and

Varian have only compatibility standards in mind, and within the set of compatibility standards only those ones for which network effects apply. Indeed, Shapiro and Varian claim findings on standards in general which may only apply to this subset. However, in this book we have the same limitation, which makes Gallagher's paper particularly interesting. According to Gallagher, "the key indicator of a dominant design is the durability or persistence of its architecture" (Shapiro and Varian, 1999b: 372). He does not define "architecture" but sees this as a much broader concept than a standard. For instance, VHS and MS-DOS are standards for VCRs and PCs respectively. VHS and MS-DOS are not seen as architectures, but VCRs and PCs are. Dominant designs can only be recognized *post hoc*, whereas standards can be identified before dominance, if any, is achieved. We think, in line with Gallagher, that a software product can be seen as a design. If it achieves dominance, it can be seen as a dominant design. In the above subsection we have argued that it can also be seen as a standard. The distinction is not as sharp as suggested by Gallagher. In the remaining part of this book we will not use the term "dominant design" but we will use some of the findings of the literature relating to this concept if we think it applies to software (for instance, Suarez and Utterback (1995) state that it generally refers to a "complete product"). We will also use the term "dominant" in cases of over 50% of market share (Anderson and Tushman, 1990).

The importance of a standard web browser and web browser standards

We have argued that a software program can be regarded as a standard. This section specifically addresses the importance of the web browser as a standard, by examining the powerful position that a proprietary standard web browser, such as IE, can have and the importance of the technical standards on which the browser is based. We will draw in particular from the noteworthy articles by Windrum.

Technical standards are essential to web browsers. The HTTP standard, for instance, allows for communicating with web servers. HTML helps the browser interpret and display documents. The Internet Protocol (IP) is used for communicating data. In this study we will not analyze such standards, which enable a web browser to function properly. One should, however, remember that a web browser is not a stand-alone product but should always be seen as part of a broader whole of standards; as one of the many complementary products (content, hardware, software, etc.) that together comprise the Internet (Windrum, 2004). The browser itself is a key component of the Internet because it represents the visual interface between the PC and the Internet. It is this vital function of a web browser – rather than the "economic rents associated with the browser production – that creates a strong incentive to gain a proprietary control of the browser technology, and hence grants possible commercial leverage over the Internet" (Windrum, 1999: 16). A company with proprietary control over browser technology could enjoy two main advantages (Windrum, 2004). First, proprietary control of the web browser technology would bring the company with the standard browser significant market power in the browser industry, yielding a potential for considerable returns, for example, by charging a price for the web browser; second, proprietary control gives significant market power. Windrum argues that market power is derived through "the control of product specification, meaning what a product is; minimum attributes, which means what it does; compatibility, which means what else it can connect with; and ergonomics, which is how a user can interface with it" (Windrum, 2004: 2). This market power can be used to leverage advantage in other, vertically related, product markets.

The latter was the aim of Netscape founders Clark and Andreessen, who planned to generate revenue through selling server software for which they could charge premium prices, rather than through browser sales (Newman, 1997). However, getting the web publishers to recognize Netscape's web browser as the standard web browser would require a large installed base to prove that Netscape's browser was indeed to be destined as the dominant standard.

Another element of proprietary control is that it allows for proprietary extension of the standard. This was one of the central issues of the 1998 United States vs Microsoft lawsuit, in which it was alleged that Microsoft used its market power to win adoption of its proprietary extensions to the open HTML standard.

The case analysis will go into more detail relating to the fight for proprietary control in the web browser market and the standardization issues involved.

Standards-setting

The literature on standards-setting distinguishes three ways, along the collaboration–competition continuum, in which industry standards can be set (Oshri and Weeber, 2006). First, there is standardization by committees or standardization bodies, meaning standards are set by collaboration; second, market-mediated standardization, which means standards are set by market competition, in which one prevails; and finally this is achieved by a combination of the two, in which case unilateral market actions, also known as the "bandwagon mechanism",[2] and negotiations are allowed (Farrell and Saloner, 1988). The GSM standards for mobile telecommunication can be seen as an example of the latter (Bekkers, 2001). As Van Wegberg (2004: 1) notes, "firms can cooperate to jointly set a standard and experiment with combinations of market process and cooperation." A hybrid standardization process can thus involve competition and cooperation in development as well as in the market.

The classification dimensions for standards and standardization are often presented in the literature as dichotomous: for example, each standard is either de facto or de jure, or either open or proprietary. In practice the classification of standards along a dimension is more a matter of degree than a simple black and white classification. Oshri and Weeber (2006) argue that standards-setting takes place more and more in a hybrid mode along the cooperation–competition continuum. They identify three main standards-setting attributes, which can vary between the two opposites of cooperation and competition (see Figure 3.1).[3]

These standards-setting attributes, which are acknowledged to "shape the manner an industry standard emerges" (Oshri and Weeber, 2006: 6), will be adopted in this study to examine the standards-setting process. Oshri and Weeber (2006: 3) define cooperative standards-setting activities as activities "that are based on negotiating a new standard, either directly with others or through standards-setting bodies and which allow access to licenses and future development" as cooperative in nature. Standards-setting activities that "represent a sole approach to set a standard in a market and that restrict access to licenses and future development" are deemed competitive in nature (Oshri and Weeber, 2006: 3).

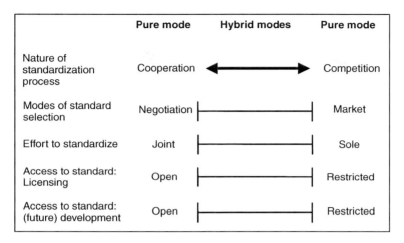

Figure 3.1   Standards-setting attributes
Source: Oshri and Weeber, 2006.

"Mode of standard selection" in Figure 3.1 refers to the manner in which a standard is set. This can be by collaboration, for example by a standards-setting body or a consortium of firms, or by market-mediation, when the outcome is determined by a standards war.

"Effort to standardize" describes the different approaches a standard-setter can follow to establish a standard. Efforts to standardize based on collaboration can involve (1) collaboration between standard-setters themselves, and (2) teaming up with third parties/complementors. In the case of OSS this could be the involvement/support of a proprietary firm in the standards-setting of an OSS product.

The last standard-setting attribute, "Access to standards," is defined by evaluating whether access to a standard through licensing agreements and participation in a further development is allowed. For example, standardization that is solely competition-driven most likely won't grant access to the standard. Because access is a key element of OSS, the next section will be devoted to an elaboration of "open standards."

Open standards

As we have already seen, standards do differ in terms of many different aspects. A vital difference between standards is the distinction between the "open" or "closed" nature of standards. Here we touch on the issue of standard ownership, standard control, and thus standard access. We consider it useful to reflect the literature on open standards and standard openness on OSS, which is all about "openness," in order to enrich thinking about open standards in the current literature by considering a new perspective of OSS as an open standard.

According to Grant (2002: 353), a standard is proprietary or closed "when a company possesses patents or other proprietary technology that gives it *ownership* and *control* of the standard." A standard is regarded as open "when a firm makes *access* to the standard open to all." Access to the standard may be free of charge, but not necessarily so. Proprietary standards are generally speaking created by an endorser who keeps control over the standard (e.g., Windows or IE by Microsoft). Proprietary standards are often protected by Intellectual Property Rights (IPR), such as through copyright or patents.

If adopted, the provider of a proprietary standard has a well-established and powerful position in the market, which can possibly be used to reap high monopoly profits. Proprietary control of the technology also allows the standard "owner" to dictate the rules under which competitors can participate in the market and to extend the standard with proprietary add-ons.

Standards cannot easily be divided into either "open" or "closed," as they encompass different degrees of openness. The term "open standard" thus means many things to many people. Microsoft, for example, claims that MS Word is open (Krechmer, 2006), much to the chagrin of open standard advocates, who complain that proprietary standards are being tagged as open. Admittedly, even the most proprietary standard is at least open to some extent to enable the supply of complementary products (West, 2004).

Standard openness can be measured in various ways. West (2004) identifies three key indicators of openness: (1) who has access to the standard; (2) goals for opening a standard; and (3) what access is provided to the standard.

Given the context of this study and the "access to standard" standards-setting attribute, the conceptual subdivision of the "access metric" is of particular relevance. West (2004) distinguishes three types of access: access to the process of creating the specification, access to the resulting specification, and access to implementations of the specification. Access to creating the specification refers to the ability to participate in creating the standard. Once a standard has been created, it is used to develop a product. In the case of a software product, the product itself and its specification are almost identical, so we can regard the software itself as the standard. Next, two categories of stakeholders may make standard implementations. Complementors can use it to produce complementary products, and competitors can produce products that can also work with the standard. Finally, customers have access to the implementation by either purchasing the product or getting it for free.

Krechmer (2006) identifies different measures of openness for different stakeholders: he argues that standard creators, implementers and users each see openness differently and have different requirements for openness. Table 3.1 provides an overview of the different requirements that the different stakeholders in different phases may consider as "open." His phases correspond more or less to West's distinction in access to the process, access to the specification, and access to the implementation.

West (2004) identifies two main reasons that make firms open up previously proprietary technology (*ex post* openness). First, a firm might want to open a standard to give in to customer pressure, or to generate support from other firms that offer complementary products for its standard: that is, to ignite network effects. Second, customers may demand open standards because they fear lock-in. Customers fear that, by committing to a proprietary standard with high switching costs to alternative products, vendors might exploit their locked-in position, for example, by asking higher prices for their products. An open standard allows multiple suppliers to offer products in which the same standard is implemented. Standards owned by companies can also be open from the start. This *ex ante* openness is normally offered to woo customers or complementors, or to establish a business for related products/services as is the case in the OSS industry.

Any company launching a new technology faces an openness/control tradeoff: they either make the necessary interfaces and specifications available to others, or reject doing so, and keep control (Shapiro and Varian, 1999b). Openness is critical when no firm is strong enough to dictate standards.

Table 3.1   Openness in different phases

	Requirements/ stakeholders	Creator	Implementer	User	Meaning of requirement
1	Open meeting	X			All may participate in the standards development process.
2	Consensus	X			All interests are discussed and agreement is found, no domination.
3	Due process	X			Balloting and an appeals process may be used to find resolution.
4	Open world	X	X	X	Same standard for the same capability, worldwide.
5	Open IPR	X	X	X	Holders of IPR contained in the standard make their IPR available.
6	Open change	X	X	X	All changes to existing standards are presented and agreed in a forum supporting the five requirements above.
7	Open documents		X	X	Committee documents and completed standards are readily available.
8	Open interface		X	X	Enables compatibility (backward and forward).
9	Open use		X	X	Relates to the assurances a user requires to use an implementation.
10	Ongoing support			X	Standards should be supported until user interest ceases rather than when implementer interest declines.

Source: Adapted from Krechmer (2006).

Openness is usually desired by new entrants, as this would allow them to overcome the installed user base advantages of the incumbent (Shapiro and Varian, 1999b). Once a company has established a dominant standard it will favor control over the standard. This allows the company to seize the advantage in terms of further developing the standard and its appropriation, for example, by licensing fees.

Sponsors of standards face several threats related to openness and control decisions. They can gain wide adoption of their standard by making it open, at the risk of not profiting from its success, as IBM did with the PC, or they can keep control over the standard, at the risk of limited adoption, as in the case of Apple's operating system (West and Dedrick, 2001).

Market acceptance of standards

Markets may demonstrate stronger or weaker trends toward achieving a common standard. In some cases, adoption of a common standard or resolution of a standards war is rapid, total and definitive, for instance, in the case of the Compact Disk versus the Digital Audio Tape (Grindley, 1995, chapter 5). In other cases, standards wars are long and "bloody," for instance, in the VCR case (Grindley, 1995, chapter 4). On the other hand, the battle between different flash memory card formats still continues and no-one has achieved dominance (De Vries, De Ruijter and Argam, 2007).

Stango (2004) notes that standards wars can arise in two basic ways. First, a new technology may come to market that is fundamentally incompatible with the old, for instance analog vs digital music recording. A second possibility is that producers could intentionally design technologies to be incompatible. Shapiro and Varian (1999a) also classify standard wars depending on how compatible each player's technology is.

Advantage in a standards war typically goes to the competitor who adopts an evolutionary strategy rather than the one who adopts a revolutionary strategy (Shapiro and Varian, 1999b).

Two important tactics typically occur in standards wars: *preemption* and *expectations management*. A preemption strategy aims to build an early lead to benefit from positive feedback (Shapiro and Varian, 1999a). It can be achieved by entering early, achieving fast-cycle product development, engaging key customers early on, and adopting a penetration pricing policy (Grant, 2002). Expectations management is all about upholding credibility and convincing and influencing potential customers and complementors that the company will emerge as the winner, as expectations tend to become self-fulfilling prophecies. To manage expectations, the standard promoter ought to engage in aggressive marketing, assemble allies and make visible commitments to the technology (Shapiro and Varian, 1999a). Another classic expectations management tactic is *vaporware*: announce an upcoming product to freeze competitors' sales (Grant, 2002). Microsoft has been accused of using this tactic on many fronts.

Standards wars can end in three ways: a truce, a duopoly, where two standards coexist, or a fight to the death, where standards compete until only one is left (Shapiro and Varian, 1999a). Shapiro and Varian identify seven key assets needed to win a standards war:

1. *Control over installed user base*: That is, control over a user base can be used by the incumbent to block rivals from offering compatible products.
2. *Ownership of Intellectual Property Rights (IPR)*: That is, software copyrights can be used to block compatibility of rival programs.
3. *Ability to innovate*: continuously enhance the standard, for example, with proprietary extensions, and make it compatible with others.
4. *First-mover advantages*: The first mover enjoys advantages in terms of experience and capturing market share.
5. *Manufacturing capabilities*: Cost advantages can help a standards producer survive or win a standards war.
6. *Strength in complements*: Availability of complements starts the bandwagon rolling and strengthens the position of the standard.
7. *Reputation and brand name*: A good reputation and well-known brand name might help convince customers that the company will win the standards war, especially in network markets where expectations are key. Microsoft, for example, has a powerful reputation which gives significant credibility among potential customers.

Standardization mechanisms

Standardization mechanisms refer to the theoretical concepts that underlie standardization in the market.[4] Classical concepts that will be discussed in this context are *network effects, positive feedback,* and *lock-in.*

In a network industry, the use of a technology becomes more valuable when its adoption, or that of a compatible technology, increases: a single fax machine is useless, but the value of every fax machine increases with the total number of fax machines in the network, because the total number of people with whom you may send and receive documents increases. An important underlying economic concept of standardization is *network effects*.[5] The concept of network effects has been applied in the literature of standards, especially where a primary concern is the choice of a correct standard (see, e.g., Besen and Farrell, 1994; Farrell and Saloner, 1985; Katz and Shapiro, 1985; Liebowitz and Margolis, 1996). The theory was originally developed for telecommunication technologies such as telephone or fax, where "the utility that a subscriber derives from a communications service increases as others join the system" (Rohlfs, 1974: 16). Network effects exist whenever "the value of a product to an individual customer depends on the number of other users of that product" (Grant, 2002: 351).

This notion relates to another important concept in the standardization literature, the *installed user base* of a product. The installed user base refers to the set of customers using the product or standard (Farrell and Saloner, 1986; Succi et al., 1998). The size of the installed user base can be of great influence to gain *critical mass*, the amount of adopters that is necessary to make it the dominant standard. The installed user bases of different but compatible products are able to interact with each other, and compatible products hence create combined network effects (Farrel and Saloner, 1985; Katz and Shapiro, 1985). Installed user base and compatibility of standards are thus tightly coupled. The firm whose standard enjoys the largest installed user base is in a strong position to define and diffuse standards, while adherence to a widely accepted standard allows a manufacturer to access an existing installed base, thereby exploiting possible economies of scale (Rohlfs, 1974).

Two main types of network effects can be identified: *direct network effects* and *indirect network effects*. Direct network effects point to the fact that increases in usage lead to direct increases in value, for example, the number of connected households increases the value of a connection to the telephone network. Indirect network effects relate to situations where increased usage of the product spawns the production of increasingly valuable complementary goods, which results in an increase in the value of the original product: for example, the more computers that are sold of a certain kind, the more software will be developed for this type of computer (Ehrhardt, 2004).

Direct and indirect network effects are known to influence software demand (Church and Gandal, 1992). Direct network externalities arise as the utility that a user derives from the adoption of a software package increases with the number of other users using that package. Software users form a two-way virtual network (Economides, 1996) through which files, documentation and knowledge flow. The larger the network is, the larger the incentive to join for potential adopters (Shapiro and Varian, 1999b). Strong indirect externalities also take place: users' decisions to adopt software depend on the number of compatible applications which, in turn, is an increasing function of software diffusion (Bonaccorsi et al., 2004). The more widespread a software, the higher the incentives for software firms and individual programmers to develop compatible applications.

Network effects give rise to *positive feedback,* also called "density dependence." If one of two or more competing incompatible standards is adopted by most of the customers and complementors, the standard that is perceived as the leading one attracts even more adoption among users and complementors who all want to be part of the "winning team." This phenomenon of a self-reinforcing cycle of success, in which "the strong grow stronger and the weak grow weaker" (Shapiro and Varian, 1999b: 175), is termed "positive feedback." Positive feedback leads to an increase in adoption of the then-dominant standard, pushing the standard even further ahead of its competitors and displaying the characteristics of "path dependence"; "later adopters' decisions depend strongly on the decisions of previous adopters" (Stango, 2004: 5).

The standard with the highest rate of adoption will in the end become dominant. Sometimes, some competing standards may continue to retain a niche position. Accordingly, markets with strong network effects are often called "winner-take-all-markets" (Ehrhardt, 2004).

The adoption of a standard is thus not in essence about quality, but first and foremost about installed user base. Katz and Shapiro (1985) argue that the *de facto* standard may be inferior to other competing technologies or standards, a premise that can be observed over and over again in technology battles, for example, in the classic Betamax vs VHS case.

The fact that users stick to a standard even if a new standard is superior may also be due to *lock-in*. In situations where lock-in exists, users are not willing to abandon the standard they have come to adopt if the costs of switching to the new standard are too significant to allow for such a change. *Switching costs* are thus the costs that are incurred when "a buyer's previous adoption choices will change the relative attractiveness of future adoption choices, making some options more expensive than others" (West, 2003b: 6).[6]

When network effects are coupled with switching costs between standards and high up-front R&D costs, Arthur (1996) predicts that the dominant technology or standard will enjoy "increasing returns to scale" that magnify an early lead in a technology contest. Such product-specific switching costs give the incumbent vendor "some monopoly power" and weaken competition between firms (Farrell and Saloner, 1988: 123). The presence of increasing returns can even give rise to situations where a small initial advantage is all it takes to favor a standard in such a manner that it gains the whole market.

Compatibility

Standards allow for compatibility between products. We have already outlined the different forms of such compatibility. Given the significance of compatibility for the program in the case under study, it seems warranted to briefly address some implications and issues that surround compatibility and standards-setting.

If software packages have to be interoperable, parts of these packages have to fit. Compatibility standards typically describe the necessary interface or specify one side in such a manner that it will fit to the other side. Applied to OSS, in order to achieve compatibility with a program, access to this program's source code is needed to be able to write an OSS program that allows for interoperability.

In general, when introducing a new product, there is often a trade-off concerning backward compatibility (Shapiro and Varian, 1999b). A product might offer backward compatibility in order to profit from an already pre-existing installed user base. On the other hand, making a product compatible with existing products, also known as the "evolutionary approach" by Shapiro and Varian (1999b), might lead to a loss in quality or performance, which would not be incurred if a superior, but not backward compatible, product was introduced, known as the "revolutionary approach" by Shapiro and Varian (1999b) (Ehrhardt, 2004).

Displacing the dominant standard?

Intriguingly, the rise of OSS contradicts the common wisdom described in the previous section: the OSS product Firefox is eroding the market share of Microsoft IE, the dominant standard in the web browser industry. A first observation to be mentioned in this context is that, in a rapidly growing market, the effect of the switching costs for the installed user base is dwarfed by the decisions of the larger population of new and potential adopters (Liebowitz and Margolis, 1990; West and Dedrick, 2001).

In general, models of the diffusion of technological innovations under conditions of increasing returns to adoption, and which are built on path dependence and lock-in (Arthur, 1989; David, 1985), predict that in the long term a single dominant technology will prevail that, once established, prevents competing technologies from obtaining a foothold in the market (Bonaccorsi et al., 2004). The models suggest that firms should either adopt the dominant standard or leave the market (Bonaccorsi et al., 2004). Still, one has to acknowledge that the software sector is experiencing a significant influx of OSS products making inroads into domains previously thought impregnable. One wonders if OSS, or more specifically Firefox, can displace proprietary software representing the dominant standard, such as IE, as happened before when IE displaced Netscape's browser as the dominant standard.[7] Bonaccorsi et al. (2004) believe that the software sector will see a final competitive equilibrium in which not one but several standards coexist.

4
Standardization Battles in OSS
A Theoretical Framework

Introduction

The current literature does not provide a framework that integrates the two domains, open source software (OSS) and standards-setting, in relation to the establishment of a dominant standard. This study aims to address this gap by constructing a framework that comprises a visualization and integration of the two domains and the three phases (development, product/standard and acceptance) of a product's route to becoming the dominant standard. The three phases will be further introduced below.

It is expected that adding these phases to the framework can help explain the interrelations between the different domains. In each of the phases, the two domains of OSS and standards-setting, each described in their own body of literature, provide two different lenses to look at the cases. Both domains introduce issues in the three phases that are expected to influence outcomes from the viewpoint of the respective domain, that is, the possible establishment of a dominant standard, and to help explain what determines observed behavior.

The structure of the theoretical framework, presenting the three phases and domains, can be found in Figure 4.1. The framework will be developed and discussed in the next section.

Adding phases to the "equation"

The standards-setting process can be considered as involving several phases. The literature shows various paths in this respect.

Domains	Phases			
	Development	Product/standard	Acceptance	
OSS				Dominant
Standards-setting				standard

Figure 4.1   Basic structure of the theoretical framework

Weiss and Spring (1992) identify three phases: the development of the standard, the distribution of the standard to the vendor and user community, and the implementation of the standard. Krechmer (2006) identifies three standardization stakeholders, namely standard creator, implementor, and user, in different periods in time. We therefore derive three phases from Krechmer's contribution as well: standard creation, implementation and use.

De Vries (2006) presents a framework consisting of six stages, namely, standard development, standard approval, making the standard available, standard's acceptance, standard implementation and use of the standard's implementation, which in essence can be reduced to standards development, making the standard available, standards acceptance, and standards use. Finally, Oshri and Weeber (2006) distinguish between a standards development and sponsoring phase.

Drawing from previous research, this study identifies three phases a software product has to go through to become a dominant standard. These phases are conceptually different and represent different phases in time. Phases are introduced to allow for in-depth analysis of linkages between issues.

The first phase, the "development phase," relates to the development of the product/standard. Once the development process has culminated in the introduction of the product to the market with the aim of becoming the dominant standard, we enter the "product/standard" phase. This phase particularly relates to the characteristics of the standard, and closely resembles Krechmer's (2006) implementation phase and the "making the standard available" stage of De Vries (2006). Finally, the third phase concerns the acceptance of the standard. It is here where "market-oriented" standards-setting activities weigh in heavily, and where competitive processes and outcomes in the market (in terms of market share, and market exit) can be observed. Depending on the outcome of the events in this last phase, the standard/product can become the dominant standard.

Identifying, positioning and defining issues in the framework

Figure 4.2 represents the theoretical framework. We will now explain the different issues of the two domains included in the framework. Each domain brings in issues related to the respective phase. Each issue can have different characteristics, for example, "quality of the product" issue can be "high" (characteristic). OSS characteristics can have different degrees and are framed in a continuum. All issues can be mapped in the framework.

Elements of the framework

OSS development

We identify two key issues related to software (and particularly OSS) and the development phase: the "origin" of an OSS product, and the development sponsorship. The "origin" of an OSS product is closely linked to the second issue: it establishes whether the OSS product is developed by the OSS community from scratch and entirely "home-grown" or whether a software product is completely based on proprietary software. OSS can also be based on parts of (previously) proprietary software. It can be argued that differences in the "gene-sis" of an OSS product will reflect on the issues of the next phase; for example, a "homegrown" software program might be of better quality because it does not have to cope with the constraints of the previously proprietary software but might at the same time lack complements and compatibility, something thought to be less likely to happen with a program that is built on parts of proprietary software.

The second issue, "development sponsorship," takes into account who "sponsors" the development of an OSS product. The issue makes a distinction between two sub-issues, "contribution" and "coordination."

Contribution covers the extent of participation of OSS development by proprietary firms. An example of a product that is completely company-sponsored would be MS Windows: all development has been done within Microsoft by Microsoft developers; on the other

Domains	Phases			
	Development	Product/standard	Acceptance	Dominant Standard *(measured by market share)*
OSS	**OSS origin:** – Homegrown vs proprietary – Software-based **Development sponsorship:** *Contribution:* – Community-sponsored vs Company-sponsored *Coordination:* – Community-sponsored vs Company-sponsored	**"Openness" of OSS program** *as stipulated by license:* – whether source code is available and modifiable; – whether OSS can be mixed with non-OSS program; – whether all derivatives must be free **Compatibility of OSS program** – between versions, – between other (OSS and non-OSS) products **Price of OSS program** **Availability of complements for program** **Quality of OSS program** (as measured by reliability, security, and features) **Availability of support for OSS program**	**Promotion sponsorship:** – OSS only promoted by commercial firm – OSS promoted by "platform" – Community sponsorship **Strategic options (Hax and Wilde, 1999):** – Differentiation/System lock-in/Total customer solution	

Standards-setting	**Standards-setting attributes (Oshri and Weeber, 2006):**
	– Mode of standard selection
	– Effort to standardize
	– Access to standard
	
	Openness (Krechmer, 2006):
	(a) Open Meeting,
	(b) Consensus,
	(c) Due Process,
	(d) Open World,
	(e) Open IPR,
	(f) Open Change
		Standards-setting attributes (Oshri and Weeber, 2006):
		– Access to standard
		– Effort to standardize
		
		Openness (Krechmer, 2006):
		(d) Open World,
		(e) Open IPR,
		(f) Open Change,
		(g) Open Documents,
		(h) Open Interface,
		(i) Open Use
			Standards-setting attributes (Oshri and Weeber, 2006):
			– Mode of standard selection
			– Effort to standardize
			– Access to standard
			
			Openness (Krechmer, 2006):
			(d) Open World,
			(e) Open IPR,
			(f) Open Change,
			(g) Open Documents,
			(h) Open Interface,
			(i) Open Use,
			(j) Ongoing Support
			
			Standards wars:
			– Two standards war tactics:
			  (1) preemption,
			  (2) expectations management
			– Seven key assets of Shapiro and Varian (1999a)
			
			Standardization Mechanisms:
			– Network effects, positive feedback, lock-in.	

Figure 4.2 Theoretical framework

hand, some OSS products, such as Linux, are completely developed by the OSS community. Between these two extremes there are situations where commercial software firms like IBM have programmers contributing to OSS projects that are not "owned" by the firm, and to which the OSS community also contributes. The extent to which these programmers and companies participate in, and the extent to which other volunteer programmers can and do participate in, the development of an OSS product is thought to influence the next phases, for example, asking a price, guaranteeing support, stipulating the openness of the program by means of a favorable license, and their outcome.

Coordination sponsorship refers to where the decision-making concerning development issues lies and what sort of entity facilitates the development of the program. Complete community coordination refers to the case in which the OSS community has full control over decision-making and in which the development is facilitated by a "community-owned/operated" clearinghouse. Complete company coordination applies when a company has full exclusive authority in decision-making, and where the development is facilitated in the company or by a company-operated clearinghouse over which it has full authority.

OSS product/standard

The relation of OSS to the product/standard phase is thought to depend on six different issues:

1. *'Openness' of an OSS product*: This issue can be considered to be the most important one. Its open nature is what distinguishes OSS from proprietary software. The degree of openness will be measured by the three distinctive issues of the open source license that governs the software : whether the source code is available and modifiable, and, if so, whether the OSS can be mixed with non-OSS, and whether all derivates must be free. These three characteristics can also be framed in an "open-closed" continuum: the most open state is when all three characteristics are open (3 × yes), while the most closed state is when all three characteristics are closed (3 × no). Complete openness is represented by the extremely open OSS GPL license, whereas the other extreme, completely closed, is represented by a proprietary license. When

the source code is available and modifiable, the program is considered to be "open" on this dimension and can be termed OSS. Whether OSS can be mixed with non-OSS is also considered to represent a certain degree of openness, where an OSS program that can be mixed with a non-OSS program is considered closed on this dimension. Finally, the case where proprietary derivatives are allowed can be regarded as less open when compared with a program in which all derivatives must be free.

2. *Compatibility*: Compatibility is differentiated in terms of compatibility between versions where complete compatibility is defined by a product that is both forward and backward compatible, and complete incompatibility refers to a product that is neither forward nor backward compatible, and also compatibility with other OSS and non-OSS products, which consists of incompatibility, two-way compatibility, inward compatibility, and outward compatibility. In the case of browsers, compatibility between other products is defined in terms of the extent the program can properly display a webpage that has been specifically written for another browser, ranging from compatible to incompatible.

3. *Price*: Is the OSS product available for free or are purchasing costs of some sort involved, for example, for manuals?

4. *Availability of complements*: Are there complementary products available?

5. *Quality*: This issue comprises reliability, security, and features, in comparison to other products/standards.

6. *Availability of support for the product.*

All the above-mentioned issues are known to play a role in defining the product and having an impact on the dominance, if any, of the OSS, and are thus included in the framework.

OSS acceptance

Two issues concerning OSS and acceptance can be identified: "promotion sponsorship" and "strategic options". OSS programs can be "promoted" on the market by an existing commercial, profit-driven company, for example, Linux by Red Hat, and Windows by Microsoft. The most pure form of community promotion is the case of the "obscure" OSS programs which are not promoted directly but can be downloaded. An OSS program can also be promoted by a less pure community form, for example, by a "platform" or organization, or by both a platform and firms together. The different forms of promotion sponsorship are expected to influence the likelihood that a product will be accepted and become the dominant standard.

The approach by which a product is promoted is related to the manner in which its sponsor competes – particularly if this sponsor is a commercial firm. The Delta model of Hax and Wilde (1999) identifies three different strategic options: System Lock-in, based on system economies; Best Product, based on product economies; or Total Customer Solutions, based on customer economies.

The issues identified above, with the exception of the "strategic options" of Hax and Wilde (1999), can be framed along a continuum, as outlined in Figure 4.3. A vertical two-sided arrow is included in the Theoretical Framework (Figure 4.2, in the right part of the OSS box) to indicate that the included issues can be framed along a continuum, with different "degrees."

Standards-setting attributes: all three phases

An important part of standards-setting are the *Standards-setting attributes* as outlined by Oshri and Weeber (2006) and explained above. We adopt Oshri and Weeber's (2006) definition of the first attribute, "mode of standard selection," where the negotiation mode refers to a case where an OSS program is selected as the standard by a standards-setting body (in the development phase), whereas the market mode refers to a situation in which the market decides which of the rival open source software programs becomes dominant in the acceptance phase. An organization or entity following a "negotiation mode" will already start to collaborate during the development phase, whereas a market mode is particularly relevant during the "acceptance phase" oftentimes leading to standards wars.

The second attribute, "effort to standardize," concerns the level of cooperation a standards-setter engages in, and relates to all three phases. Collaboration can occur between standards-setters themselves, and third parties (e.g., complementors). The "effort to standardize" is particularly relevant to the development and acceptance phases. In the development phase, entities can either collaborate or compete, as in the "acceptance phase."[1] More specifically, collaboration in the acceptance phase can be between the OSS community and commercial firms, or between commercial firms.

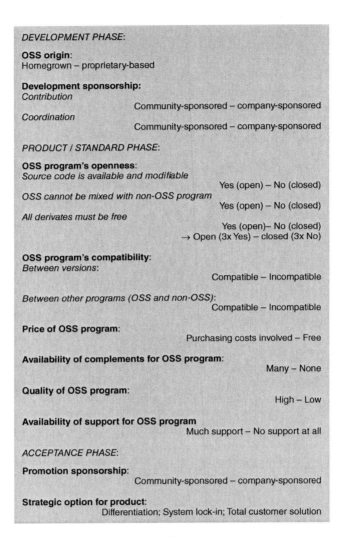

Figure 4.3   Continuums for OSS issues

In the acceptance phase, it refers to collaboration in promotion in whatever form.

The last attribute, "access to standard," consists of two dimensions: (1) access to a standard; and (2) possibility of future contribution to development. In the development phase, access to standard particularly relates to access to the development process and whether future participation in the development of the standard is allowed. In the product/standard phase it relates to whether the source code is available, whether it can be changed, whether it can be mixed with other programs, and so on.

Openness requirements: all three phases

The openness requirements of Krechmer (2006) offer an insightful specification of and addition to Oshri and Weeber's (2006) "access to standard" attribute. These requirements will therefore be added to the framework.

Krechmer identifies three stakeholders (creator, implementer, and user) throughout the standards-setting process, each with different openness requirements. This study takes Krechmer's reasoning a little further by deriving three different phases from the stakeholders: creation, implementation, and use. These phases are then equated with the phases of our theoretical framework: "creation" with "development"; "implementation" with "product/standard"; and "use" with "acceptance." It should be noted that, although the phases in the framework have strong resemblance to Krechmer's phases, they are conceptually not completely the same.

The "openness requirements" listed in the acceptance phase have a strong resemblance to the issues identified for the OSS – product/ standard box in the framework (e.g., both boxes cover "support"). The contribution of Krechmer's requirements in the acceptance phase lies in illuminating user preferences for openness that might further a standard's acceptance. Hence, it places a strong emphasis on user preferences, contrary to the issues defined for the OSS – product/standard box, which deals with the characteristics of the product/standard as such.

Standards-setting: acceptance phase

Standards-setting in the acceptance phase is captured by the standardization mechanisms discussed above. We will examine whether the adoption of the standard is influenced positively or negatively by network effects, positive feedback, and lock-in. In the acceptance phase, a standards war may emerge. Standards wars are captured by Shapiro and Varian's (1999b) two standards war tactics, namely, preemption, and expectations management and by the seven key assets introduced above.

The presence of one or more of these tactics, assets and standardization mechanisms is expected to be of influence on the likelihood of the standard becoming the dominant standard.

Dominant standard

In the end, the standards-setting in the acceptance phase, and the influence of OSS thereon, can result in the establishment of a dominant standard. The dominance of a standard is measured by the share of the installed user base the standard holds, as outlined above. In the case of web browsers, the installed user base is comprised of all PCs with a web browser installed and used. A standard's share of the installed user base is measured by the *usage market share* for that particular standard (browser).

Identifying interlinks by applying the framework

Besides mapping and evaluating the relevant issues, the theoretical framework also allows for identifying and reflecting on assumed interactions. Two kinds of direct influences or interlinkages can be identified: horizontal interactions within the *domains* that explain outcomes of an *individual* case, meaning whether the product/standard becomes dominant or is accepted to a certain extent, and vertical interactions, within the *phases*, that explain how the first domain influences the second domain by comparing *two cases:* a case in non-OSS proprietary context and a case in an OSS context. Figure 4.4 visualizes these possible manners in which issues can interact by the use of horizontal and vertical arrows.

Domains	Phases			
	Development	Product/standard	Acceptance	
OSS				Dominant standard
Standards-setting				

Figure 4.4   Potential direct influences/interlinkages

Notes:

→ = inter-domain interactions: possible influence of issues on outcomes.

↓ intra-domain interactions: possible influence of OSS on standards-setting.

Interrelation on the inter-domain level
(between phases): explaining outcomes

The horizontal arrows explain the outcomes of *individual cases*. Horizontal arrows also examine which issues of the respective domains explain the outcomes, meaning the *key influencers*. In this regard, these key influencers could be some OSS characteristics, but could also be standards-setting issues. After identifying the key influencers, these will be examined across the different phases.

So, by interrelating the OSS software characteristics with the standard-setting mechanisms, we hope to explain how the characteristics of development, product/standard, and acceptance *related to OSS* explain the adoption of a standard, and how the characteristics of development, product/standard, and acceptance *related to standards-setting* explain the dominance of a standard.

Interrelation on intra-domain level (in phases):
explaining the influence of OSS on standards-setting

The vertical arrows explain the possible influence of OSS on standards-setting. To analyze the influence of OSS on standards-setting, one has *to compare two cases* to examine whether issues related to OSS change standards-setting. To this end, characteristics for OSS and standards-setting have to be mapped for the respective phases for a case involving an OSS product and, to compare, a case involving a non-OSS product. By applying the theoretical framework, characteristics of both the "non-OSS" case and the "OSS case" can be mapped and evaluated.

A subsequent comparison of the characteristics of the two cases for the respective domains and phases can identify changes, differences and similarities. It can then be examined how differences in characteristics for OSS issues for that particular phase explain differences in standards-setting characteristics for that particular phase, in order to draw a conclusion on the assumed influence of OSS on standards-setting. So, by interrelating on the intra-domain level and by comparing two cases, this study aims to identify what changes, and how differences in the characteristics of development for OSS explain differences in the characteristics of standards-setting in the development phase, the product/standard phase and the acceptance phase, respectively.

Interrelation on general level (indirect)

Besides this direct vertical influence of OSS on standards-setting, there is also expected to be what we term an indirect relation. This relation can be examined on a general level by comparing the key influencers of outcomes of the first case, which is a non-OSS standards battle, and the second case, which is based on a standards battle involving OSS. By comparing the two cases on a general level, we can examine whether there is a difference in key influencers, and if so, whether this difference can be attributed to OSS.

Applicability of the framework

The theoretical framework does not only allows the analysis of standards-setting and competitive dynamics surrounding the establishment of a dominant standard. It can also be used to examine the development and introduction of a new version of an already pre-existing software product/standard. This is indicated by a horizontal two-sided arrow above the three phases.

Although the framework is specifically constructed to take the OSS element into account, it can also be applied to a non-OSS context.

5
Industry Background

This chapter provides an overview of the industries involved in the standardization battle between IE and Firefox. We first describe the PC industry and the software industry, followed by a case description of the web browser industry.

The PC industry

The computer industry finds its origins in the late 1950s, when IBM started producing mainframe computers. These complete proprietary systems were offered by a few vertically integrated companies such as IBM and DEC (Ehrhardt, 2004).

The age of the personal computer (PC) commenced with the introduction of a fully assembled micro-computer in 1976 by Apple. It was not until 1980 that IBM, the then leading producer of high-end mainframes, started developing PCs. The IBM PC was based on an open architecture, and the production of the key components was outsourced to other companies (Bresnahan and Greenstein, 1999). The open nature of the PC created a whole related industry of new firms specializing in the production of individual PC-related components, for example, hardware parts or software, which proved to be a huge boost for the computer industry (Chandler, 1997). The IBM PC itself and the features and technical standards it was built on quickly became the industry standards,[1] and in 1992 IBM enjoyed a market share of over 90% (Ehrhardt, 2004).

IBM's success was, however, not sustainable. Its open architecture, once the very driver that had spurred adoption of its PC, now

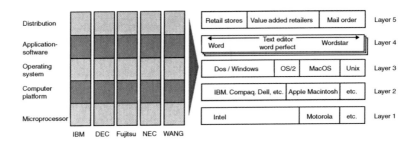

Figure 5.1   Transformation of the PC industry
Source: Ehrhardt, 2004.

undermined the foundations of IBM's PC business by significantly lowering the industry's entry barriers. With the ready availability of all components of IBM's PC, companies like Compaq and Dell began to produce IBM-compatible PCs; the PCs essentially became commodities. IBM suffered badly from the subsequent price competition and shifted focus to its service business.[2] In 2005, IBM sold its PC division to the Chinese PC manufacturer Lenovo.

Nowadays HP has established itself as the PC industry's biggest player with a 19.2% worldwide market share for the third quarter of 2006, followed by Dell with 14.6% and Acer with 7.9% (Gaudin, 2007).[3]

Figure 5.1 provides an overview of the vertical "pre-PC" industry structure and the horizontal structure that followed from the introduction of IBM's PC. Nonetheless, it should be noted that Apple still adopts a vertical approach. The rise of the PC and related products and services helped set off a wave of innovations and enterprises that now encompass the Information Technology (IT) industry. The current IT industry, the outer limit of this study's unit of analysis, can be categorized into four market segments: hardware products, hardware maintenance services, software products and services, and Internet and processing services (Hoch et al., 2000), as outlined in Figure 5.2.

The software industry

The software industry generally is regarded as having its origins in the mid-1960s, when there was an increasing need for software to go

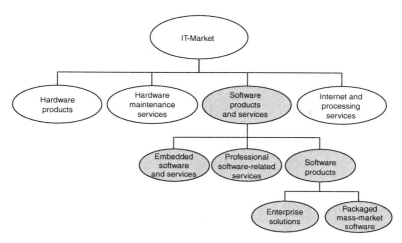

Figure 5.2 Structure of the IT industry
Source: Hoch et al., 2000.

with the computer mainframes. The concept of "the software product," in which one firm developed the program and subsequently sold it to a second firm for use on that firm's computer, first originated because of the increasing complexity of software and the shortage of labor needed for each firm to make its own software (Mann, 2004). A crucial event that can be considered to be the main impetus for the rise of software was the decision of IBM in 1968 to "unbundle" its software from its hardware. From that point on, sales of software products grew rapidly (Haigh, 2002).

McKinsey and Co. (1999) found the following characteristics of the software industry:

1. Entry barriers are low: relatively little capital is needed; firms therefore face a continuous threat of new entrants.
2. High fixed costs for research and development, but, once developed, the marginal costs for producing a software package are low.
3. There is a race for leadership, and a tendency to concentration to create network effects.
4. An established market position in the industry is never stable because of new technologies.

Contrary to the mainstream views, Mann (2004: 8) argues that there is an "astonishing lack of concentration in the software industry – a facet that has considerable implications for the competitive structure of the industry and its openness to innovation". He notes that intense coverage of Microsoft's seeming dominance of the industry has clouded the fact that the industry is populated with a large number of significant but not monopolistic commercial players.[4] In fact, the top ten software companies in terms of revenue represent less than 30% of the industry revenues at large (Mann, 2004). The lack of concentration seems to be supported by the variety of products and niche markets, in which no company can have total market power altogether.

As shown in Figure 5.2, the software industry can be divided into three segments: Software Products, Professional Software Related Services, and Embedded Software and Services.

Professional Software Related Services consists of IT services and IT consulting. Embedded software describes software that is part of a product or service, and which is not sold separately, for example the program on a cell phone.

Software Products can be further subdivided into Enterprise Solutions and Packaged Mass Market Software. Major products in the Enterprise Solutions segment are ERP, CRM and SCM packages. For Packaged Mass Market Software, two distinct markets can be identified: the server market and the desktop market. Within these segments one can differentiate between Operating Systems and Applications.[5]

Applications, in which category the web browser can be classified, can be differentiated into horizontal and vertical applications (Ghosh et al., 2002). Microsoft enjoys practically a monopoly in horizontal applications with its Office suite. Other companies offering horizontal applications are Sun, OpenOffice and Corel.

The web browser industry

A web browser is "an *application program* that provides a manner to look at and interact with all the information on the *World Wide Web*".[6] In other words, it is the program used to surf the Internet.[7]

Web browsers communicate with web servers via HTTP (Hyper Text Transfer Protocol) to download web pages as well as to submit information to the web servers. A webpage's content is typically stored in the HTML (Hyper Text Markup Language) file format. The first web browsers only supported a simple HTML version. The rise of proprietary web browsers such as Internet Explorer and Netscape Navigator led to the development of non-standard HTML extensions (leading to interoperability problems between website and browser). Currently, web browsers support the standards-based HTML and XHTML, which display web pages in the same manner, regardless of the browser.

Some of the current popular browsers include additional components such as a web editor, an e-mail Usenet client, or an IRC client. These browsers (e.g., Internet Explorer) are often referred to as (Internet) suites rather than simply web browsers.

Overview of the web browser industry's origins and evolution[8]

The origins and rise of the web browser are inextricably bound up with the Internet revolution. The Internet started as a collection of academic and government institutions sharing information via text. In 1991 Tim Berners-Lee of CERN created the first web browser, the WorldWideWeb,[9] which allowed browsing and viewing text pages on other PCs in the network and laid the foundation for the Internet boom.[10]

We will now provide a short overview of the web industry's evolution prior to Browser War I. This evolution can be captured in two different phases in time: the emergence of the browser, and Netscape's dominance.

The emergence of the browser (1991–1994)

With the November 1993 launch of the NCSA's Mosaic,[11] the first graphical browser, the Internet's popularity greatly increased. Other browsers had been developed after 1991, for example ViolaWWW and Midas, but their adoption was limited to specific niches: it was Mosaic that brought the Internet to the general public. Mosaic was originally designed and programmed for UNIX's X Window System. It was developed at NCSA by Marc Andreessen and Eric Bina. Development of Mosaic started in December 1992. Version 1.0 was released on April 22, 1993, followed by two maintenance releases during summer 1993. Version 2.0 was released in December 1993, along with version 1.0 releases for both the Apple Macintosh and Microsoft Windows.

The Mosaic browser was considered a "killer application" because it was the first browser to offer a polished multimedia graphical user interface. It further introduced support for sound, video clips, forms support and history files, and enjoyed cross-platform operability.[12] The licensing terms for NCSA Mosaic were generous for a proprietary software program. For all versions, non-commercial use was generally free, with certain limitations. In addition, the X Window System/ Unix version publicly provided source code. Source code for the other versions was made available under certain conditions. However, Mosaic was never released as OSS.

In mid-1994, Marc Andreessen quit the NSCA to co-found Mosaic Communications Corporation. The company was renamed Netscape Communications Corporations to resolve legal issues with NCSA. In August 1994, NCSA assigned Mosaic's commercial rights to Spyglass Inc., which subsequently licensed a reworked version of its own technology to several other companies that wanted to create their own commercial browser, including Microsoft, which used the technology for its first version of Internet Explorer.[13] Mosaic's popularity as a separate browser dried up with the release of Netscape Navigator. The NCSA consequently stopped developing Mosaic in January 1997.

Netscape dominance and Microsoft's awakening (1994–1995)

Netscape Navigator 1 was released in December 1994. The new browser improved much on Mosaic's usability and reliability and immediately took over the browser market. It captured more than 60% of the market in less than six months after its release. By December 1995, Netscape Communications Corp. was worth $7billion (Yoffie and Cusumano, 1999).

Navigator's quality was a large factor in its success. Another contributing factor was Netscape's "free but not free" concept in which fully functional versions of Navigator could be downloaded for a free trial period (Cusumano and Yoffie, 1999). Users were then asked, but not required, to pay $39 per copy. The main sources of revenue were the Netscape server software packages, for which the company charged up to $50,000. Clark and Andreesen understood that in order to sell their server software they had to build up a large installed user base, thereby locking the market into their particular Web browser (Windrum, 2004).

Microsoft was late to recognize the potential of the Internet. The company started to show the first signs of its awakening with the May 26, 1995 "The Internet Tidal Wave" memo by Bill Gates, in which he declared that the Internet is "the most important single development since the IBM PC" (Business Week, July 15, 1997: 3), and in which he pushed Microsoft to respond to the "Internet tidal wave" by developing software for the web. In this memo, Gates further called for integrating the browser and MSN into Windows, and working with Netscape customers, including MCI, newspapers and others who were considering Netscape's products (Andrews, 1997).

In December 1994, Microsoft licensed Spyglass's browser technology to help it quickly and easily develop a web browser. Microsoft's first browser, Internet Explorer 1, was released in August 1995 as part of the Windows 95 Plus package, but it was not yet bundled with the operating system. A new version, IE 2, was released in November 1995, but it did not impress when compared with Netscape.

On December 7, 1995, the 53rd anniversary of Pearl Harbor Day, Microsoft CEO Bill Gates made a moving speech to analysts, journalists, customers and Microsoft employees, in which he acknowledged that Microsoft had been lax to recognize the opportunity of the Internet and the threat Netscape posed but that it would be Microsoft's Number One priority from that moment on. Gates pledged that "from now on Microsoft will embrace and extend the Internet". The "Pearl Harbor Day speech" and Microsoft's subsequent actions signaled the beginning of a browser war, taking on Netscape, which had more than 80% market share, but from which Microsoft would emerge victorious.

Market share data

In general, market share is understood as a firm's unit sales volume (in a market) divided by the total volume of units sold in that market over a particular time period. In this "classical interpretation," market share numbers only apply to current sales, and they do not take into account the pre-existing users, which the concept "installed user base" does. In the case of browsers, market shares might be measured in terms of the share in number of downloads. However, a download does not mean that the browser is actually used, in particular if the browser is available for free. Therefore, usage share would be a far more accurate approach of measuring than download counts, as it reflects the number of people who (1) have downloaded the browser, (2) have installed it, and (3) are using it to view websites.[14] A single download can also be installed on many PCs, while one user can also be responsible for multiple downloads. Therefore, browser market shares can be best measured in terms of their global usage shares, which are often measured by the installed user base: "the percentage of daily Internet users worldwide that access the Internet through a particular browser" (Statmarket.com).[15] Shapiro and Varian (1999b: 29) note in this respect: "An unusual but handy aspect of the browser market is that the market shares can be measured in terms of usage rather than purchases of the product, since web sites can determine the browser used by a visitor. For the purposes of assessing network externalities, usage is far more important than purchase: the active installed user base is what matters". This study will therefore make use of browser usage shares provided by web metrics firms, as they seem to be the most accurate representation of the market share of a web browser, and are released on a regular basis, so that a comparison can be made. This study does not differentiate between different versions of the same browser in measuring market share.

There are two basic approaches to measuring a browser's market share. The first and most common and popular one is to check browser logs at websites to see what percentage of the website's visitors uses which browser. This is how web metrics firms like Xiti[16], Net Applications, WebSideStory, and OneStat, using different samples, derive market share estimates for the web browser industry.[17] The second approach amounts to surveying users. The Netcraft surveys[18] are well-respected in this approach. Figure 5.3 provides an overview of the worldwide market share of the different web browsers. The source is Xiti.com[19], and the data as of October 31, 2007. The data do not distinguish between different versions, if any, of the same browser.

Internet Explorer clearly dominates the market, with Netscape having almost disappeared, and there is an increasing market share for Mozilla Firefox. The Opera and Safari browsers are niche players, whose market share oscillates around 1 and 2%.

Market share varies by continent and country. Data for Mozilla Firefox, September 2007, are as follows: Asia 15.4%, Africa 15.6%, South America 18.6%, North America 20.4%, Europe 27.7%, and Australia

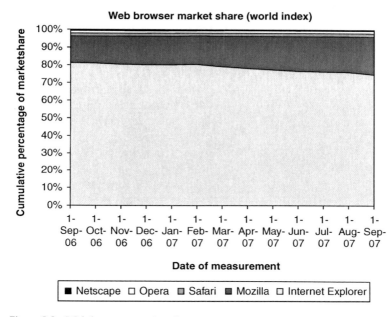

Figure 5.3   Web browser market share
Source: Adapted from Xiti.com.

and Oceania 30.3%.[20] Within Europe, the largest market shares for Firefox can be found in countries near the former Iron Curtain: Finland 45%, Slovenia 42%, Poland 41%, Slovakia 41%, Hungary 38%, Czech Republic 37%, and Estonia 37%. The lowest market shares for Firefox, 16%, were found in the United Kingdom and in The Netherlands.

Figure 5.4 provides data from another source, period 2002 until 2007. According to this source, Internet Explorer dominated in July 2007, with 84.33% of the web browser market, while Firefox held 12.79%, and the remaining browsers 2.51%. The source is Onestat. com, and the data as of July 2, 2007.[21] According to this source, Mozilla's Firefox global usage share is still growing.[22]

Making a market share picture for a longer period, including Browser War I, is only possible by combining data from different sources, which has the risk that these are not entirely comparable: see Figure 5.5.

See the Appendix for more market share data. The proliferation of more or less conflicting browser statistics made it difficult to exactly

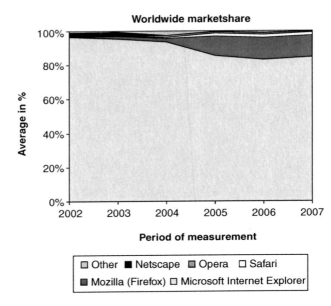

Figure 5.4 Worldwide market share

Note: Figures underlying this graph can be found in Appendix D.

Source: Adapted from Onestat.com

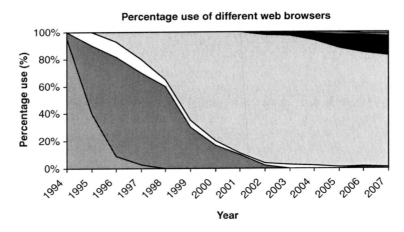

Figure 5.5 Overview of market share of main web browsers 1994–2005

pinpoint Firefox's market share, but the overall picture is that it is steadily increasing, at the cost of IE. The market shares of other browsers are very limited.

Taking into account the multiple reports that all estimate Firefox's share to be between approximately 12% and 15% or even more, achieved in a rather short period of time, and the apparent continuing growth of its market share, it seems warranted to state that a new browser war, Mozilla Firefox versus Microsoft Internet Explorer, is upon us.

Trends in the web browser industry

A November 2005 article by the Financial Times pointed to a new wave of Internet development, the so-called Web 2.0. This wave is driven by small start-ups at the grass-roots level where low key start-ups are able to produce innovative software more easily than before (Nuttall, 2005). Software development is less costly than it used to be because applications can be speedily constructed with the help of freely available building blocks of OSS (Nuttall, 2005).

Microsoft has recognized this threat. In a memo to staff, Bill Gates cautioned that this phase of online innovation "will be likely to be very disruptive to the industry's established powers" (Nuttall, 2005: 1). Gates even likened the memo about the new breed of companies to his "Internet Tidal Wave" memo of ten years earlier. Tim O'Reilly, an OSS proponent, has commented that competing with this wave of innovation will pose a fundamental business challenge Microsoft did not face with Netscape, as at that time – and contrary to the current situation – the battle was still framed across a software application (Nuttall, 2005).

Examples of Web 2.0 are technologies like Ajax, which is a loose bundle of technologies to create interactive web pages; RSS, an approach of distributing information on the Internet at the user's request; Wikis, communal web pages that can be changed by anyone who has access; and Blogs.

Another development is the use of applications and services over the web, rather than using them as pieces of software loaded on PCs. Companies like Salesforce.com already provide services over the Internet.

Another trend is the emergence of the mobile browser market. Currently, this market is dominated by Opera Software ASA's Opera Mini, related to Apple (Keizer, 2007).[23]

The web browser industry's main players

Microsoft

Every day over one billion people all over the globe use Microsoft's products (Cushman and Sanderson King, 2003). Founded by Bill Gates in 1975, the company is now the world's largest software enterprise. Its most popular products are the Windows operating system and the Office applications suite, which both have an almost ubiquitous position in the desktop market. Other Microsoft software products include Windows NT server, Windows CE, a handheld computer operating system, Windows Mobile software, and SQL database OS (Cushman and Sanderson King, 2003). Microsoft also has stakes in non-software markets, such as the MSNBC cable TV network, the MSN Internet portal, Microsoft Encarta, and the home entertainment market, where it markets Xbox and Zune.

Cusumano and Selby (1995: 127) identify five critical success factors for Microsoft:

1. Enter evolving mass markets early or stimulate new markets with good products which can become the industry standard.
2. Continuously improve products incrementally, and periodically make old products obsolete.
3. Push volume sales to ensure that products become and remain the industry standard.
4. Leverage the industrial standards to develop new products and market linkages.
5. Integrate, extend and simplify products and services to reach new mass markets.

Microsoft invests huge amounts in research and development to catch technology's next waves to "up the ante" with its competitors, and to further develop its existing products. In 2006 only, Microsoft spent $7.5 billion on R&D[24] (Infoworld.com, May 31, 2006), dwarfing the $1.22 billion spent by Google[25] (Google, 2006).

Microsoft has been listed on the Fortune 500 since 2007. The company employs about 79,000 employees and has global annual sales of $51.12 billion for the 2007 fiscal year (Microsoft Annual Report).[26]

Microsoft and competition in the web-browser market

On October 1, 2004, at an appearance at the Computer History Museum in northern California, Bill Gates, when asked about a possible threat from Linux, was quoted as replying: "Microsoft has had competitors in the past. It's a good thing we have museums to document this stuff" (Corcoran, 2004). Microsoft indeed has a history that seems to warrant Gates' statement. The company has proven to be very apt at weathering the storms of change in the software industry and staying ahead of competitors. The company may not always be the first to venture into a new technology, but when it does, it often succeeds in becoming the most dominant market player. In fact, as Microsoft insiders have put it, "at any given time Microsoft has lagged behind in networking, desktop technologies, online services, Internet technologies and web browsers. And yet the landscape is littered with the bones of Microsoft's competitors" (Baker, 1998: 41). MIT professor Cusumano observes that Microsoft's history is "based on seeing emerging these mass markets and throwing masses and masses of resources at them before the trend peaks" (Waters, 2005: 1).

Microsoft's domination of the industry is further supported by the huge base and monopoly position of its operating systems and applications in which consumers have invested substantial financial resources and time (Consumers Federation of America and Consumers Union, 2002). The dominance of Microsoft is strengthened by the fact that Microsoft's products are sold pre-installed with most PCs, and many users buy a bundle of hardware, operating system and applications (Hoch et al., 2000). It can be argued that Microsoft invests in Internet Explorer primarily to indirectly benefit its Windows operating system in order to maximize its positive externalities (Wang et al., 2005: 160).

Having once enjoyed the advantages of an open standard, Microsoft ensures that its products will not suffer the same fate as IBM's "open standard" PC. The company aggressively competes to sustain its dominance and control.

In the mid-nineties, the company saw its dominant position threatened by the Netscape/Java (Sun) tandem, whose "middleware"[27] was inserting itself between the Windows operating system and the applications that run on it (Consumers Federation of America and Consumers Union, 2002). The Netscape/Sun alliance aimed to turn the browser into an operating system by developing a Java-based, cross-platform browser that would be located on top of the operating system and take over the functions of that operating system (Windrum, 2004).

Microsoft foresaw that the rise of middleware as espoused by Netscape and Sun could result in a multi-platform strategy, where the "applications barrier to entry" would be dramatically lowered (Consumers Federation of America and Consumers Union, 2002). If a substantial number of Internet-related applications were developed to run on Netscape's browser, Navigator (in combination with Java software from Sun) could become an alternative platform. Microsoft would then face competition from any operating system that worked with Navigator (Klein, 2001). As Bill Gates remarked: "A new competitor 'born' on the Internet is Netscape. Their browser is dominant, with 70% usage share, allowing them to determine which network extensions will catch on. They are pursuing a multi-platform strategy, where they move the key API[28] into the client to commoditize the underlying operating system" (quoted in Consumers Federation of America and Consumers Union, 2002: 19).

A Netscape-based operating system would pose a grave threat to Microsoft's operating system business, as is outlined in the 2002 attachment to the Tunney Act Comments on the Microsoft–Department of Justice Proposed Final Judgment by the Consumers Federation of America and Consumers Union (2002: 24):

> If a competitor of Microsoft can create a stock of compatible applications, he can advertise that the new operating system can run all the existing programs, undermining the economic leverage of Windows. If the installed base of platforms and browsers are out there, the Windows operating system could be bypassed. By capturing the browser market, however, Microsoft precluded that possibility. The campaign against Netscape simultaneously extended the monopoly into the browser market and defended the monopoly in the operating system market by preserving the barrier to entry.

Browser War I was therefore much more than a competitive battle for web browser market share: for Microsoft it was a battle for dominance in the operating system market as well. In the case description below, more information about Microsoft in this respect will be provided.

Following Microsoft's competitive actions, which led to a reversal of Netscape's fortunes, Jim Clark of Netscape asked the US government to "investigate Microsoft's market position for employing its monopolistic position in the PC OS market to leverage its increasing market share in Internet browsers and servers" (Cushman and Sanderson King, 2003: 63).

On May 18, 1998, the US Department of Justice (DOJ) and 20 US states filed charges against Microsoft, stating that Microsoft illegally abused its monopoly power.[29] Microsoft was accused of "predatory pricing," meaning deliberately lowering prices to kill competition, of tying IE to Windows 95, and of making "exclusionary contracts" where companies such as Compaq were forced to sign contracts that would prevent them from using any browser other than IE (Ehrenhaft, 2001: 73–74).[30]

On April 3, 2000, the court ruled in favor of Netscape's claims, directing that Microsoft had to be split into two companies (Walker, 2001). In June, part of the ruling (about the Microsoft split-up) was overturned by another court, and on September 6, 2001, the Justice Department announced that it would seek a settlement. This settlement was reached on November 2, 2001. It prevented a break-up of Microsoft but imposed a number of other restrictions. The Department also ordered Microsoft to share its API with other companies, but did not demand that Microsoft stop tying other software with Windows in the future (BBC.com, November 2, 2001).[31]

Over the 1990s, Microsoft engaged in several other practices that some deem to be monopolizing. These include: (1) preventing the developers of applications from sharing information about its operating system with other firms; and (2) licensing its operating systems to the OEMs on the basis of the number of PCs sold, irrespective of whether they carried Microsoft's operating system. The US courts subsequently commanded Microsoft to allow its application software developers more flexibility in sharing information about its operating system with other firms, and instructed the firm to change its OEM licensing practices (Gupta et al., 2005). Recently, not only in the US but also in Europe, action has been taken to prevent the dominance of Microsoft in not sharing information. Microsoft lost a court case in which it had to pay a fine of $690 million after an antitrust ruling in 2004 (BBC News, 2007),[32] and an additional $400.8 million in 2006 for non-compliance (Lawsky, 2007).[33]

Microsoft and OSS

The OSS's influence on the competitive landscape of the software industry seems to be increasingly profound and lasting. Microsoft in particular faces a many-headed enemy, whose new approach of writing software speeds up the pace of innovation and threatens Microsoft's business model (BBC.com, May 9, 2005).[34]

Interestingly, Dedrick and West (2004) note that Microsoft has actually unintentionally stimulated many companies and developers to engage in OSS projects, as this has proved to be the most viable way to compete with Microsoft. Netscape's decision to release its source code, following its defeat by IE, endowed OSS with corporate credibility and visibility, whereas IBM's and HP's backing of Linux was inspired to counter Microsoft in the server market.

Following the embrace of Linux by these companies, the operating system now enjoys increasing adoption. Several European institutions have opted to install Linux, while several Asian countries such as China, South Korea and Japan actively push for Linux solutions (BBC.com, May 10, 2005).[35] Other OSS intruders are also attacking non-operating system parts of the Microsoft empire, such as OpenOffice and MySQL, on the applications side.

A 2003 report by Forrester Research (quoted in Frost, 2005), found that 81% of the IT managers and executives surveyed believed that OSS will to some degree affect Microsoft, and of those 81%, the most popular answer from four options on how this would take place was that Microsoft would have to reduce prices.

Microsoft officially identified the popularity of OSS as a danger in a 2003 SEC filing, in which it outlined that "to the extent the open source model gains increasing market acceptance, sales of the company's products may decline, the company may have to reduce the prices it charges for its products, and revenues and operating margins may consequently decline" (eWeek.com, February 3, 2003).

The company has, however, for a long time acknowledged the threat OSS can pose to its dominance. The so-called Halloween documents offer a unique insight in this respect. These documents refer to a series of confidential Microsoft memos on potential strategies related to OSS and to Linux in particular. The first Halloween document was leaked to OSS advocate Eric S. Raymond in October 1998 (around Halloween), who immediately published an annotated version on his web site.[36] Microsoft has admitted the documents' authenticity, but stated that this particular document concerned "an engineer's individual assessment of the market at one point in time, not Microsoft's official position" (CNET News. com, November 6, 1998).

We now cite some key points of the memo to analyze how Microsoft (or one of its engineers) regarded Linux in particular and OSS in general, and the strategies it proposed to neutralize this threat:

1. "Recent case studies provide very dramatic evidence…that commercial quality can be achieved/exceeded by OSS projects."
2. Open source software "is long-term credible…FUD tactics[37] can not be used to combat it".
3. "Linux can win as long as services/protocols are commodities."
4. Microsoft should "De-commoditize protocols and applications" (Raymond, 1998a).

The Halloween memos suggest that Microsoft was very concerned about OSS and Linux in particular. It foresaw that, if they were left unchecked, Microsoft would have difficulty in competing for developer mindshare, software quality, and resources available for R&D.

The memos also contain sections on other OSS threats such as the Mozilla browser. However, at the time the memo was written, the writers were right to state that the browser in its then form would not pose a threat in any manner to Microsoft IE.

The memo further observes that OSS is based on open standards/ protocols. Consequently, the memo suggests that Microsoft should de-commoditize protocols and applications (quote 4): "OSS projects have been able to gain a foothold in many server applications because of the wide utility of highly commoditized, simple protocols. By extending these protocols and developing new protocols, we can deny OSS projects entry into the market." (Raymond, 1998b). This strategy to respond to the OSS threat has been termed "embrace and extend" and is a tactic powerful companies often engage in. The strategy aims to neutralize the OSS threat by inventing new standards and embracing and extending current open standards with proprietary additions. In this manner, OSS may very well not be able to use these standards, thus denying OSS market entry. In any case, the OSS program will most certainly not enjoy the same, extended functionality that its proprietary counterpart offers, thus limiting the OSS's attractiveness.

If successful, Microsoft here effectively changes the "rules of the game" so that the competition has to play by the "rules" of Microsoft. The alleged effectiveness of "embrace and extend," nicknamed "embrace, extend and extinguish" (Wang et al., 2005), lies in network effect.[38] In the first edition of his book *The Road Ahead*, Bill Gates actually explained in detail his plans to use the network effect to Microsoft's advantage.

In 2003, Microsoft launched the "Get the facts on Windows and Linux" marketing campaign, in which Windows was compared favorably to Linux. This campaign seems to be aimed at labeling Linux as being software developed by amateur volunteers, and at implying that it seems inexpensive but is far more expensive in the end (BBC.com).[39]

On its "Compare Windows vs Linux" website[40], Microsoft also cites reliability, security, performance, intellectual property indemnification and interoperability as reasons to prefer Windows above Linux. This, however, did not prevent IBM from backing Linux, and Microsoft's claims are disputed by OSS advocates.

In July 2003, Microsoft rather imitated the OSS movement by starting the Shared Source Initiative, which allows certain approved governments and corporations to access most of the Windows source code, and by granting access to less vital parts of the code to all developers.

Although Microsoft denied the Shared Source Initiative was a response to Linux[41], it conceded that "Microsoft has been learning from the OSS community regarding the benefits of deeper collaboration and increased transparency leading to better communication with customers" and that "With more than 80 source code offerings being used by more than two million developers, Microsoft is looking to apply the best of open source while helping its customers avoid many of the model's pitfalls."[42]

Another contribution to the competitive dynamics of the software wars between Microsoft and OSS was the paper *Dynamic Mixed Duopoly: A Model Motivated by Linux vs. Windows* by Casadesus-Masanell and Ghemawat (2006), in which they describe "a dynamic mixed duopoly model" in which a profit-maximizing competitor such as Microsoft interacts with zero-price competition, for example, Linux. Casadesus-Masanell and Ghemawat argue that neither Windows nor Linux is likely to be forced out of the market: Microsoft has too much market share and OSS offers too many benefits for users to be pushed out.

Mozilla

Mozilla was the original code name for the product that came to be known as Netscape Navigator, and later, Netscape Communicator.[43] It was also the name of Netscape's first alligator-like mascot.

In 1998, Netscape decided to release the source code of its Communicator web browser, to benefit from input from the OSS developer community. The development of the browser's source code was moved to an open source project, called the "Mozilla Project." Following the source code release (to be described in more detail in the next chapter), Mozilla.org was created to act as a clearinghouse for contributions by developers from both within and outside Netscape.

Due to constraints on part of the original source code, a new rendering/lay-out engine,[44] called Gecko, was excised out of Mozilla and combined with the XUL user interface language[45] to create a leaner, faster Mozilla browser (CNET News.com, April, 16, 1998).

In July 2003, AOL laid off the employees of its Mozilla open source browser team. The Mozilla Foundation was subsequently created to carry on the open source Web browser work of the Mozilla project. Time Warner, AOL's mother company, pledged $2 million in funding for the new foundation (CNET News, July 15, 2003). The Mozilla Foundation provided organizational, legal, and financial support for the Mozilla open source software project. The Foundation used the name "Mozilla" as "the principal trademark representing the Foundation and the official releases of Internet client software developed through its open source project".[46] In 2005, the Mozilla Foundation spun off the Mozilla Corporation, a for-profit, taxable subsidiary for product development, marketing, and distribution of Mozilla products.[47] Mozilla Corporation relies on a core group of employees, as well as input from a large community of worldwide contributors, and is a wholly owned subsidiary of the Mozilla Foundation. In 2006, Mozilla had 25 employees; in 2008 the number has grown to 120 (many of these are hires from the community of volunteers; volunteers still develop 40% of the code) (Mendonca and Sutton, 2008).

The foundation's first product, the Mozilla Application Suite, a.k.a. Mozilla 1.0, was released on June 5, 2002. The integrated applications suite included a browser, an advanced e-mail and newsgroup client, an IRC chat client, and an HTML editor.[48] The most well-known products released by the Mozilla Foundation are, however, two offspring from the Mozilla Suite: the email program Thunderbird, and the web browser Firefox.

The Firefox project started out as a branch of the browser component of the Mozilla Application Suite. Renamed Phoenix, then Firebird, the browser was finally introduced as Mozilla Firefox. Firefox has since become the Mozilla foundation's main development focus, along with the Thunderbird email program, and has replaced the Mozilla Suite as the Foundation's official main software release.[49] The Suite is unofficially superseded by SeaMonkey[50], an Internet suite based on the source code of the Mozilla Suite, to be further developed and released by the Mozilla community.

Firefox has attracted attention as an alternative to other browsers such as Microsoft Internet Explorer. Since its release on November 9, 2004, Firefox has contributed to a reduction in Internet Explorer's dominant usage share. After the 1.0 release, it took Firefox only 99 days to reach 25 million downloads, and 334 to reach the 100 million mark by October 19, 2005, making it one the most downloaded OSS programs ever.[51] Firefox 1.5, released on November 29, 2005, set a new record, being downloaded more than 1.5 million times on the day following its release (ZDNet UK, December 1, 2005). See Table 5.1 for an overview of the download counts for Firefox 1.0 in October 2005. On February 2, 2006 the download count for Firefox 1.0 and 1.5 combined was about 120 million. Recently, on December 3, 2007, more than 125 million active users were claimed by Firefox.[52]

Table 5.1 Downloads of Firefox 1.0.x from Mozilla website since November 9, 2007, based on web log Asa Dotzler: http://weblogs.mozillazine.org/asa/ archives/2005/11/more_than_two_m.html, November 2005.[53]

Date	Downloads (millions)
November 10, 2004	1
February 16, 2005	25
April 29, 2005	50
August 14, 2005	80
September 20, 2005	90
October 19, 2005	100
August 1, 2006	200[a]
February 16, 2007	300[b]
September 7, 2007	400[c]

Source:
[a] Betanews.com, last accessed December 8, 2007; http://www.quickonlinetips.com/archives/2006/08/mozilla-firefox-browser-crosses-200-million-downloads/, last accessed January 8, 2008.
[b] http://www.quickonlinetips.com/archives/2007/02/mozilla-firefox-tops-300-million-downloads/, last accessed January 8, 2008.
[c] http://www.news.com/8301-13580_3-9773836-39.html, last accessed January 8, 2008.

Other Mozilla initiatives are Camino, a Web browser project for Mac OS X, and a calendar project. Mozilla code is also used in Netscape 6 and 7. Firefox 2.0 was released in October 2006, and Firefox 3.0 is planned for the first quarter of 2008 (Cabello, P., Mozillalinks, November 24, 2007).[54]

6

Browser War I (1995–1999)
Microsoft Versus Netscape

Two cases will be reviewed in this book. The first case is the browser war between Microsoft and Netscape. A special attention is given to the source code release by Netscape, as that laid the groundwork for Mozilla Firefox. Browser War II between Mozilla and Microsoft will be described in the next chapter.

Internet Explorer development phase

In reaction to Netscape's success, which was 80% market share by summer 1995, Microsoft arranged a meeting with Netscape, in which it offered Netscape the option of either entering into a special relationship with Microsoft and developing only non-Windows browsers, or being regarded as a competitor (Jenkins et al., 2004). Netscape declined the offer of a partnership. Microsoft consequently launched its own web browser Internet Explorer(IE) 1 (August 1995) and IE 2 (November 1995).[1] The original IE 1.0 browser code was licensed from Spyglass, but the Microsoft team quickly changed the original codebases and practically rewrote the browser from scratch for IE 3.0.[2] The first two IE product cycles occurred within a very short span of time, and allowed the browser to gain a little ground against Netscape.[3]

New versions of IE and Netscape Navigator, later known as Communicator, were released at a rapid pace in the years following Bill Gates's declaration that Microsoft was "hardcore" about the Internet. See Table 6.1 for an overview of the releases of different versions of IE and Netscape Navigator/Communicator. Microsoft

Table 6.1 Browser War I timeline (1994–1999)

1994	
December	Release of Netscape Navigator 1.0
1995	
April	Netscape launches Navigator 1.1
August	Microsoft launches IE 1.0
November	Microsoft launches IE 2.0
December	Pearl Harbor speech by Bill Gates; Netscape holds an estimated 80% market share, against about 3% for IE
1996	
February	Netscape launches Navigator 2.0
August	Microsoft launches IE 3.0 Netscape 3.0 is released
1997	
June	Netscape launches Communicator 4.0
August	Netscape offers stand-alone browser Navigator 4.0
September	Microsoft launches IE 4.0
November	Dataquest reports that Netscape's market share in the past year has fallen from 73% to 53% while IE's share has risen from 20% to 39%
1998	
January	Netscape makes Navigator and Communicator available for free and announces that it will release the source code of its browsers
March	Source code is posted on Mozilla.org
October	IE overtakes Navigator and Communicator in market share
November	Netscape 5.0 canceled in favor of a new product, based on a new technology (Gecko) AOL buys Netscape
1999	
March	Microsoft releases IE 5.0

Source: Adapted from Yoffie and Kwak, 2001.

only started to approach Netscape's technical superiority with the release of IE 3.0 in August 1996.

The software giant made considerable amounts of resources available to win the browser war. For the development of IE 4.0, the IE team had over 1,000 people, almost as many people as Netscape had in their entire company. From 1995 to 1997, Microsoft invested more than $100 million per year in web browser development (Klein, 2001). These investments clearly helped Microsoft to increase the quality of IE relative to Navigator. The estimated development costs for Navigator rose from $2 million for version 1.0 to about 20 times that amount by 1997–1998, while Netscape's development team grew from a dozen developers to more than a hundred (Yoffie and Kwak, 2001). IE 4.0, launched on October 1997, sealed the end of Netscape's dominance. This browser offered superior performance and features, and quickly dethroned Netscape Communicator as the most popular web browser.

Internet Explorer product/standard phase

Quality

The release of the Netscape Navigator 1.0 signaled the start of the "mass consumer browser" era as we know it today. Netscape Navigator's easy interface and new features attracted scores of new users. IE 1 (August 1995) and IE 2 (November 1995) provided little that persuaded Netscape users to defect: Netscape simply offered a superior browser, and kept improving. With its newest version, Netscape 2.0 (March 1996), Netscape introduced breakthrough features (Java, frames, JavaScript plug-ins).[4] It further added a full mail reader called Netscape Mail, thus transforming Netscape from a mere web browser to an Internet suite. For the later versions of Netscape, Netscape relied on Firefox, as they used the Firefox as its core.

With the release of Internet Explorer 3.0 (August 1996), Microsoft made a first step towards improving the quality. The browser offered some features Netscape Navigator also offered while also innovating in new areas (CSS[5] support and VBScript).[6] However, IE 3.0 could not be considered as technologically superior to Netscape 2.0 (Cusumano and Yoffie, 1998; Shapiro and Varian, 1999b).[7]

Netscape 3.0 (August 1996) introduced mouse-overs and many other new features.[8] The release of the fourth generation browsers marked a turning point in the browser war. Netscape launched its Communicator 4.0 in June 1997. The new suite included the Navigator web browser as well as other components. Internet Explorer 4.0 was launched shortly afterwards, in September 1997. It can be regarded as a significant leap forward for Microsoft. IE 4.0 finally met (or exceeded) most of the capabilities of its rival's browser.[9] The new IE browser received favorable reviews in PC magazines and was considered to be better than Netscape 4.0, which suffered from a series of bugs. Another drawback was that Netscape's code engine was not functioning well, and could not handle another update.[10] IE 4.0 was also faster, was the first browser to support the W3C's CSS, could reflow a page, and its DOM[11] implementations were better too.[12]

IE 4.0, like its counterpart, included several additional components. An important change was the introduction of Active Desktop, whose single interface allowed for managing both files stored on the hard drive and documents on the web (Yoffie and Kwak, 2001). This new feature clearly foreshadowed the integration of the browser and operating system that Microsoft intended.

This integration took more shape with Microsoft's new Windows 98 operating system, which tightly integrated IE's code into the code of the operating system. Unlike Netscape, which regarded the browser as "a graphical interface that could sit on top of Windows or any operating system, Microsoft wanted the browser to be an integral part of its operating system" (Yoffie and Kwak, 2001: 8).

The release of IE 5.0 (March 1999) was the final blow to Netscape's aspirations. IE 5.0 was the first browser that supported large parts of the W3C's DOM, supported CSS and was superior to any browser Netscape could manage to offer at that time.[13]

Price

In contrast to Netscape, Microsoft kept IE and the accompanying Internet Information Server completely free of charge, even for business customers. Netscape requested modest charges for corporate users of the Netscape browser. Netscape Navigator copies were freely available to special sectors of users (e.g., teachers, students), and 90-day evaluation copies of the browser could be downloaded without restrictions or costs. After the free trial period users were asked but not required to pay $39 per copy (Yoffie and Cusumano, 1999).

Compatibility and standards

During the browser war, it was common that a website included a "Best viewed in Netscape" or "Best viewed in Internet Explorer" button. These logos were indicative of the divergence between standards supported by the respective browsers, and of the absence of interoperability between websites and browsers.

Both Microsoft and Netscape liberally incorporated proprietary extensions to open standards like HTML in their browsers, to gain an edge by product differentiation (Windrum, 2004). The result was that a website designed for IE displayed differently (or not fully) when viewed with Netscape, and the reverse (Yoffie and Kwak, 2001).

Since both Netscape's and Microsoft's browsers had previously exclusively supported their own DOM, interoperability problems were multiple. In order to be cross-browser compatible, large parts of the website's HTML code had to be rewritten for each browser to be supported. A common DOM promised to greatly simplify the development of complex web applications. To this end, W3C DOM Level 1 was proposed in October 1998 (CNET News, January 9, 2003).[14] The standardization effort did not cause an immediate improvement, as noncompliant browsers such as Internet Explorer 4.0 and Netscape 4.0 were still widely used.[15]

A significant step forward for IE was the acceptance of the Cascading Styling Sheets (CSS). CSS is a language that lets designers separate the visual definition of a web page or site from its content. This allows very elegant and flexible styling that guarantees reliability in all modern browsers, and that can be modified – or even changed completely – quickly and consistently without affecting the content. It is designed primarily to enable the separation of document structure, written in HTML or a similar markup language, from document presentation, written in CSS. The CSS specifications are maintained by the W3C.[16] CSC was proposed by Microsoft to W3C, in which standards body it participated, over Netscape's JavaScript Style Sheets (JSSS). Only Netscape Communicator 4 supported JSSS. Soon after Netscape Communicator's release in 1997, Netscape stopped promoting JSSS, instead focusing on the rival CSS standard. CSS greatly simplified the design of websites and a website's accessibility (CNET News, October 9, 2003). Microsoft disclosed CSS to the W3C for free. In 1999 it obtained a patent for the technology.[17] Microsoft's browsers were initially only available for Windows 95. With the release of new versions, it gradually introduced support for other platforms such as Macintosh (IE 3.0) and UNIX (IE 4.0).

Internet Explorer acceptance phase

Microsoft's rise and Netscape's demise

Netscape responded to Bill Gates's Pearl Harbor speech by improving its browser through incorporating technology from other firms such as Adobe Systems (Corts and Freier, 2003). Following Gates's statement, IE's market share grew, but did not come close to that of Netscape.

Since mid-1995, the general public had begun to take notice of the Internet, mostly using Netscape Navigator, which was the *de facto* standard at that time. In June 1996, Netscape announced that the installed user base for Navigator had reached over 38 million users (Corts and Freier, 2003). Netscape Navigator 2.0 (March 1996) was succeeded by Netscape Navigator 3.0 (August 1996). IE 3.0 was released on August 12, a week before Navigator 3.0. Microsoft reported more than 1 million downloads of IE 3.0 in its first week (Yoffie and Kwak, 2001). By the end of 1996, Netscape's market share had declined from 87% to 70%, while IE's market share had risen from 4% to 24% (Corts and Freier, 2003).

The increase in market share for IE can be related to the fact that Microsoft was bundling IE with the Windows 95 OS (released in August 1995), of which 45 million copies were expected to be launched in 1996 alone (Corts and Freier, 2003).

In April 1996, in the internal memo "Winning the Internet platform battle," Microsoft executive Brad Chase highlighted the important role of web developers. Noting that "content drives systems," Chase urged Microsoft "to make sure that the best web applications and content becomes available to IE users first. Microsoft must reach out to a new type of partner, the webmasters. They are the ones who actually create the web sites" (Corts and Freier, 2003: 3). Due to the proprietary nature and extensions of both browsers, the same web page code often looked different when read by any browser other than the one it was designed for. Web publishers had to choose for which browser they would design their page. They would design a page for the browser that was thought to become the one with the most adopters so that their websites could be viewed by the largest possible number of people. To win the browser war, Microsoft would thus have to become the webmaster's preferred browser. To spur webmaster adoption of IE, the company offered FrontPage, which allowed for easy web design of IE optimized websites. Microsoft also made its website server (Internet Information Server) available for free. This profoundly affected Netscape because its revenues largely came from selling servers.

Microsoft further fueled the adoption of IE by making deals with Internet Service Providers (ISP) such as AOL to include IE as default browsers for their subscribers, who were mostly first-time Internet users. In particular, the deal with AOL, a company with 5 million subscribers, was a significant step in boosting IE's adoption. To bring AOL on board, Microsoft even went as far as to agree to put an AOL icon on the Windows 95 desktop, thereby sacrificing its own Microsoft Network.

By the end of 1996, Microsoft had struck deals with about 2000 ISPs. Microsoft also moved aggressively to persuade PC makers to include IE rather then Navigator. Microsoft enforced these office equipment manufacturers to sign a contract which obliged them to install IE and *not* any other browser. Given the fact that IE was free and Windows 95 was shipped with about every PC in the world, PC makers would think twice about trading the free IE of the mighty Microsoft for a non-free Navigator of the less powerful Netscape. The PC makers could not afford not to distribute Windows and therefore they had to sign this contract. Finally even Mackintosh signed such a contract (Bresnahan and Yin, 2007). Microsoft also formed partnerships with major resellers (Yoffie and Kwak, 2001).

The release of IE 4.0 (September 1997) and Communicator 4.0 (October 1997) did not change Netscape's fortunes: IE continued to gain market share. To retain its market share, Netscape announced a new initiative by forming 100 industry partnerships. Its new partners agreed to package the Navigator 4.0 browser, unbundled from the Communicator Suite, with their products.[18]

By the end of 1997, Netscape's market share amounted to about 50%. The once successful company found itself at the brink of losing this dominant position.

Netscape's source code release

Netscape suffered badly from Microsoft's competition and not only in terms of lost market share. The company reported slowing growth and its first quarterly operating loss ever ($88 million for the last quarter of 1997) in early 1998. In response to these difficulties, Netscape cut back in its development program and reduced its staff. For the long term it undertook two initiatives to regain market momentum.

First, Netscape declared all Navigator and Communicator versions to be completely free (Netscape Press Release, January 22, 1998). It further released the Communicator 4.0 source code to other developers for customizing and enhancement: developers would thus be able to modify the Communicator code for their own products; in return they were required to submit their changes or contributions to Netscape, which would then have the right to incorporate these modifications into its next version of the browser. The move was not least inspired by a White Paper written by Frank Hecker in which he argued for the release of Netscape's source code.[19] Hecker's paper in turn drew heavily on the "Cathedral and Bazaar" concept of Eric Raymond.[20]

Netscape CEO Barksdale believed that open source development of the browser would help Netscape compete with Microsoft: "By giving away the source code for future versions, we can ignite the creative energies of the entire Net community and fuel unprecedented levels of innovation in the browser market. Our customers can benefit from world-class technology advancements; the development community gains access to a whole new market opportunity; and Netscape's core businesses benefit from the proliferation of the market-leading client software" (Netscape Press Release, January 22, 1998). Netscape further hoped that the source code release, coupled with free copies of standard versions of Communicator and Navigator, would help boost its browser market share along with sales of its server software (CNET News, March 31, 1998).

An internal Netscape team guided the release of the source code.[21] Eric Raymond was invited to a day-long strategy conference on February 4, 1998 with some of Netscape's top executives and technical people.[22] Together they designed Netscape's source-release strategy and license. On February 23, 1998, Mozilla.org was created to facilitate the open sourcing of Netscape's source code, and to function as a clearinghouse for contributions by developers from both within and outside Netscape. On March 31, 1998, Netscape's Communicator source code was finally posted on Mozilla.org.

Mozilla.org's clearinghouse function allowed for the assembling of the necessary components into Mozilla browser, which would be available for free from Mozilla.org. Netscape would release its own version of this browser branded as Netscape Navigator, which would be available for free from netscape.com.

Besides open-sourcing its browser, Netscape also started to place a greater emphasis on sales of server applications and corporate services. Communicator 4.0, which combined the Navigator browser with workgroup-collaboration features, was specifically designed to appeal to corporate customers. Another initiative was the enhancement of the so far undercapitalized Netcenter, an information and commerce service built around the heavily visited Netscape.com web site, from which Netscape hoped to reap advertising fees.

The open sourcing of its browser, however, did not help to turn the tide: Netscape kept losing market share to IE. In October 1998, IE overtook Communicator in market share. In response, Netscape accused Microsoft of unfair business practices and filed a series of complaints with regulatory bodies; these efforts helped to persuade the US Department of Justice to undertake a broad investigation of Microsoft under antitrust statutes.

End of Browser War I

The Browser War I effectively ended in 1998 when it became clear that Netscape's downward slide in market share was irreversible. In November 1998, Netscape announced that it would cancel Netscape 5.0 in favor of a browser based on the new Gecko code base. In the same month, the Internet giant America Online (AOL) purchased Netscape for $ 4.2 billion. AOL's interest in Netscape was mainly thought to be that, by acquiring Netscape, it could become less dependent on the IE web browser. The acquisition further helped the company to get its hands on Netcenter, Netscape's web portal, and by that time one of the most popular portals worldwide.

In the years following, Netscape's market share further slipped away. In 2002, IE controlled an estimated 90% of the browser market (Corts and Freier, 2003). IE, the victor of the browser war, had established a seemingly impregnable position as the dominant web browser.

Internet Explorer adopters and reasons for adoption

In the first period of the browser war, Netscape users would cite the browser's quality and its multi-platform operability as reasons for adoption. When Microsoft introduced IE, Netscape had a superior product, and a huge installed user base. Microsoft, on the other hand, had its reputation, resources, and control of the operating system. Besides, the Internet was just starting to be discovered by the mainstream in 1995. The existing browser installed user bases were soon dwarfed by the influx of Internet novices, people new to the Internet, who were using a browser for the first time. These people were mostly using IE, simply because this browser was preloaded on their PCs or on the CD-ROMs of their ISPs. These inexperienced users would spare themselves the hassle of downloading and installing Netscape, as long as IE was preinstalled and worked well.

Windrum (2000: 7) notes that "of the 7,000 respondents contacted by the 8th GVU World Wide Web Survey in autumn 1997, 72% stated they had never switched browsers. 81% of new users (defined as users with 12 months or less experience of the Internet) stuck with the first browser they came into contact with. The report suggests this rigidity is not due to difficulties in learning how to use a rival browser or to differentiate between product features offered by rival browsers. Instead, users are, in general, simply unwilling to invest time in searching for, and testing, alternative browser software. Moreover, new users' inexperience of the Internet appears to make them uneasy with even the idea of downloading software (including rival browsers) over the Internet." Research by Bresnahan and Yin (2007) shows that the majority of IE users were new users who got IE pre-shipped; there was hardly any shift from one browser to the other. The IE use among Mackintosh users was limited; they hardly switched to IE as new and better versions came out. This changed after Microsoft and Apple signed a contract to pre-ship IE 4.0.

In general, there did not seem to be a clear distinction between the browser adoption behavior of firms and individuals, although in the final stages of the browser war, when it was clear that IE was going to be the dominant standard, companies were backing away from Netscape and opting for IE. After version IE 4.0, Microsoft's browser was regarded as superior, and after the disastrous launch of Netscape 5.0, a considerable number of professional Netscape users switched to IE.

Evaluation and summary of characteristics of IE in Browser War I

OSS characteristics

OSS origins: IE is a proprietary-based program. The first two versions of IE were based on external technology from Spyglass. For version 3.0, IE was rewritten from scratch.

Development sponsorship: Both the coordination of the development of IE and the contribution towards the development of IE were completely company-sponsored; the program was developed within Microsoft.

OSS program openness: The program was closed source code, not available or modifiable, so could be termed proprietary.

OSS program's compatibility: IE is backward compatible with its preceding versions. Due to the proprietary additions to IE and Netscape, the browser was somewhat incompatible with Netscape; pages written for Netscape could be viewed by IE, but were not displayed correctly, and vice versa. The web browsers were expected to follow standards set by W3C, but competition and innovation led both IE and Netscape to extend the existing standards with proprietary features.

Price of OSS program: IE has been free since its introduction.

Availability of complements for OSS program: A number of additional add-ons were available. The most important complement is the Windows operating system.

Quality of OSS program: Upon introduction of IE 4.0, IE was considered to be of lesser quality than Netscape. From IE 5.0 on, IE is regarded as clearly technologically superior to Netscape.

Availability of support for OSS program: Since it was promoted by a large company with experience in product support, much support could be offered.

Promotion sponsorship: Promotion sponsorship can be characterized as company-sponsored (with Microsoft as the sponsor). It should be noted, however, that Microsoft also entered into alliances with other firms to promote IE.

Strategic option: In the terms of Hax and Wilde (1999), Microsoft used "System Lock-in competition". By integrating IE with Windows, Microsoft made the operating system an important complement to the browser. This was an essential part of Microsoft's vertical integration strategy, in which Microsoft software products are connected to Windows in order to help Windows gain more users to dominate the operating system market (Economides, 1997, cited by Wang et al., 2005). Another important complement was the Internet content, which was increasingly optimized for IE. Contributions of complementors in the broader IE environment created lock-in to

IE's advantage, locked out Netscape, and left IE as the dominant proprietary standard.

Figure 6.1 shows an evaluation of the OSS characteristics for IE. IE's position on the continuum is indicated by its logo.

Standards-setting characteristics

The standards-setting process by which a web browser can become the dominant standard can be evaluated by looking at several attributes and concepts.

We will now evaluate the standards-setting attributes of Oshri and Weeber (2006) against our case. Table 6.2 provides a summary of the attributes for the different phases.

Mode of standard selection: Market mode: the market has decided on the adoption of IE.

Effort to standardize: The efforts to standardize pursued for IE were solely for development and Microsoft did not collaborate with third parties or rival standards-setters. There was some collaboration in the product/standard phase in which Microsoft participated in W3C. In the acceptance phase there was again some collaboration as Microsoft entered into agreements with ISPs and OEMs to get IE adopted.

Access to standard: Access to the development process was closed, like the access to the product whose source code was not available.

Openness: In terms of Krechmer (2006), IE is closed for 8 of his 10 requirements; for "Open World" and "Open Interface" it is partly open.

Table 6.2 Standards-setting attributes: collaboration – competition

	Development phase	Product/ Standard phase	Acceptance Phase
Mode of standard selection	–	–	Market mode (Competition)
Effort to standardize	Sole	Some collaboration	Collaboration
Access to standard	Closed (Competition)	Closed (Competition)	–

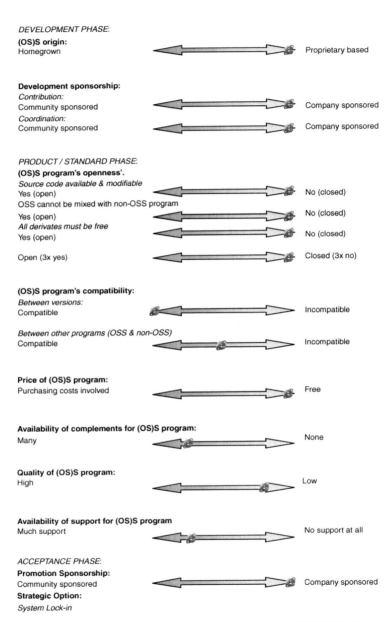

Figure 6.1   OSS characteristics of IE in Browser War I until 1997, IE 3.0

Note: IE (until 1997).

Standards-war tactics: IE was not the first browser. Netscape enjoyed a significant head-start, and IE could therefore not pre-empt the browser market. Microsoft did, however, pre-empt the distribution channel level by using exclusive agreements with ISPs and OEMs at the expense of Netscape, which only had the Internet distribution channel left.

The expectations management tactic was also used by Microsoft, for example, when it announced that it was to launch its own browser to defeat Netscape and signaled to the market that it was "hardcore" about the Internet, and that it was going to win this war. ISPs and OEMs therefore were given a signal that required them to decide which "winning team" they wished to bet on. Microsoft further stated early on that it planned to integrate IE into Windows, which would make it more difficult for Netscape to convince users who overwhelmingly used Windows that they needed Navigator (Shapiro and Varian, 1999b).

Seven key assets: We will now briefly elaborate on the seven key assets needed to win a browser war, as identified by Shapiro and Varian (1999a). We indicate IE's advantageous or disadvantageous position versus Netscape on each of these assets.

1. *Control over installed user base*: Both IE and Netscape had control over their installed user bases by adding proprietary additions; however, IE was more successful in doing so.
2. *Ownership of IPR*: Both Microsoft and Netscape owned the IPR of their browsers.
3. *Ability to innovate*: Microsoft's ability to innovate was low for the first three versions of IE. However, versions 4.0 and later were considered of better quality and more innovative than Netscape's products.
4. *First-mover advantages*: Netscape was the first mover, and enjoyed an installed base of over 80%. Second mover Microsoft managed to come up with an improved version (IE 3.0) before Netscape did (Navigator 4.0) (Breshnahan and Yin, 2007).
5. *Manufacturing capabilities*: Microsoft had a vast number of talented developers and enough money to support development.
6. *Strength in complements*: On top of the add-ons by third parties, Microsoft could leverage its strong position in the operating system market.

7. *Reputation and brand name*: Both Microsoft and Netscape were well-known.

Table 6.3 summarizes the above findings.

Standardization mechanisms: The web browser industry at the time of IE can be characterized as having strong network effects, and lock-in.

1. *Network effects:* There are strong network effects due to the incompatibilities of the browsers/web pages.[23]
2. *Positive feedback*: Positive feedback for the incumbent product was not decisive. On the contrary, IE grew stronger and the previously dominant Netscape lost market share. It was only after a while, when it became clear that IE was set to win the browser war, that positive feedback was starting to work in IE's favor.
3. *Lock-in*: Yes: the increase in adoption of IE was due to users who were new on the Internet, and for whom IE was their first browser. Netscape users also stuck to their browser.

All individual tables can now be integrated into the framework: see Figure 6.2.

Table 6.3   Seven key assets of Shapiro and Varian (1999a); IE relative to Netscape

Seven key assets	IE relative to Netscape*
1. Control over installed user base	$+-$
2. Ownership of IPR	$+-$
3. Ability to innovate	$-$
4. First-mover advantages	$--$
5. Manufacturing capabilities	$++$
6. Strength in complements	$++$
7. Reputation and brand name	$+-$

Notes: $*++$, strong advantage; $+-$, neutral/no advantage or disadvantage; $-$, disadvantage; $--$, strong disadvantage.

Domains	Phases			Dominant standard
	Development	**Product/standard**		
OSS	**OSS origin:** Proprietary based **Development sponsorship:** – *Contribution:* Company sponsored – *Coordination:* Company sponsored	**"Openness" of OSS program** Closed **Compatibility of OSS program** – *Between versions:* Compatible – *Between other (non-OSS) products:* Somewhat incompatible **Price of OSS program:** Free **Availability of complements for program:** Many (including the Windows OS) **Quality of OSS program:** Mostly low **Availability of support for OSS program:** Much support available	**Promotion sponsorship:** Company-sponsored **Strategic option:** System lock-in	
Standards– setting	**Standards-setting attributes:** – *Effort to standardize:* Sole – *Access to standard:* Closed **Openness (Krechmer, 2006):** Closed	**Standards-setting attributes:** – *Effort to standardize:* Joint – *Access to standard:* Closed **Openness (Krechmer, 2006):** Closed	**Standards-setting attributes:** – *Mode of standard selection:* Market – *Effort to standardize:* Joint **Openness (Krechmer, 2006):** Closed **Two standards war tactics:** – *Pre-emption:* Yes (esp. in distribution) – *Expectations management:* Yes **Seven key assets (Shapiro and Varian, 1999a):** (relative to IE): – *Positives:* Manufacturing capabilities; Strength in complements; Control installed user base – *Negatives:* Ability to innovate; First-mover advantages – *Neutrals:* Ownership of IPR; Reputation and brand name **Standardization Mechanisms:** – *Network effects:* Yes – *Positive feedback:* No – *Lock-in:* Yes	**Dominant standard** *Yes, finally.*

Figure 6.2 Overview of characteristics of IE in Browser War I

7
Browser War II (2003–2008)
Mozilla Versus Microsoft

This chapter describes Browser War II, between Mozilla and Microsoft. While Browser War I took place in the past, Browser War II is still in the making. In this book we describe the events up to the end of 2007, with the hope of updating this book in the future.

Mozilla Firefox development phase

Microsoft dominance and Mozilla inaction (1999–2003)

Microsoft emerged as victor from Browser War I and promptly rested on its laurels, rarely upgrading the IE browser. IE 6.0 was released in 2001, and Microsoft waited five years until it launched IE 7.0 in March 2006. Neither Microsoft nor Mozilla released browsers that contained important innovations.

After having released the source code, Netscape proceeded to work on Communicator 4.5. However, it did not take long to become clear that the Communicator 4.0 codebase was not suitable for open source development and that it was a hindrance to the development of an advanced browser. The Netscape codebase, originally written for Netscape Navigator 1.0 and upgraded through the years, was furthermore widely considered to be inferior to the one used in Microsoft Internet Explorer. It was slow, did not comply well with W3C standards, had limited support for dynamic HTML, and lacked features such as incremental reflow.

To address these shortcomings and to enable future innovations, Mozilla's code base had to be rewritten from scratch. The open source community's focus therefore subsequently shifted to the development of a next-generation browser that would be based on the new Gecko codebase. There is more about this codebase in the next section.

It took the Mozilla project more than 4 years to release the first official Gecko-based browser, Mozilla 1.0, in May 2002. Meanwhile, the market share for IE by that time commanded approximately 80% or more of the browser market, with Netscape trailing far behind.[1]

After Microsoft had been found guilty in the anti-trust case brought against it by the DOJ, Netscape sued Microsoft for damages (*CNET News*, January 22, 2002). In May 2003, the companies reached a settlement: AOL/Netscape agreed to drop charges against Microsoft from which in return it received $759 million in damages, and a 7-year royalty-free IE (*CNET News*, May 29, 2003). AOL licensing IE for another 7 years was by many considered as the final nail in Netscape's coffin.

On July 15, 2003 Time Warner, then parent company of AOL, split up Netscape. Most of the programmers working on Mozilla were fired or reassigned. Large parts of the Netscape Enterprise Suite were acquired by Red Hat, which subsequently announced that it planned to convert the suite into an OSS product to be bundled with Linux.

The Mozilla Project spun off in the Mozilla Foundation, which was on the same day formally registered as a not-for-profit organization, and has become from that day on the main steward of Mozilla's development. The Foundation received $2 million in funding from Time Warner, and took on many of Netscape's ex-employees (*CNET News*, July 15, 2003).

Table 7.1 provides a timeline of Browser War II.

Gecko, Mozilla's engine

Development of the Gecko layout engine, the most important subset of the browser's code base[2], had already started at Netscape in 1997. The new layout engine was developed in parallel with the old one, with the intention being to integrate it into Netscape Communicator when it was mature and stable. After the launch of the Mozilla project, Gecko – whose development was mainly carried out by Netscape employees (MacCormack et al., 2004) – was released under an open source license. Originally unveiled as Raptor, and later rebranded by Netscape as Gecko, it was further developed by the Mozilla community

Table 7.1   Browser War II timeline (2001–2007)*

2001	IE 6.0 is released.
2002	
June	Mozilla 1.0 is released.
2003	
July	AOL lays off the employees of its Mozilla open source browser team; the Mozilla Foundation is created.
2004	
November	Firefox 1.0 is released.
2005	
April	Firefox market share is estimated at 6–8%.
May	Netscape releases Netscape Browser 8.0.
July	Microsoft releases a first beta version of IE 7.0.
August	Mozilla Corp. is created.
October	Firefox achieves 100 million downloads.
November	Firefox 1.5. is released; Firefox market share estimate at 8–10%.
2006	
January	Google announces Google Pack, a free software package to include Firefox.
March	IE 7.0 is released. Additionally, it includes a phishing filter and a new GUI redesign.
October	Firefox 2.0 is released. It includes also a phishing filter and GUI redesign, as well as a spell-checker for text fields and several other new features.
2007	
September	Firefox achieves 400 million downloads.
October	Microsoft drops the requirement for Windows Genuine Advantage for Internet Explorer 7.
November	Netscape Navigator 9.0 final is released. Firefox 3.0 beta 1 is released.

Note: *2001 should here not be understood as the start of the browser war.

and became a main part of the code base for Mozilla-based browsers from that moment on.[3] Gecko is cross-platform, which enables it to work on a number of different operating systems, including Microsoft Windows, Linux and Mac OS X. It is designed to support open Internet-related standards such as CSS 1/2, the W3C Document Object Model, XML 1.0, RDF, and JavaScript.[4]

In October 1998, Netscape announced that its next browsers would be based on Gecko, and development on Netscape 5 was subsequently halted. The first Netscape release to incorporate Gecko, Navigator 6 (Netscape 5 was never used), was released on November 14, 2000, based on Mozilla 0.6 source code. This browser was, however, far from stable, which alienated many loyal Netscape users. Later versions of 6.0 were much better, but did not impress. In August 2002, Netscape released Netscape 7.0 (based on Mozilla 1.0.1). This version was a direct continuation of Netscape 6 with very similar components, so it did not help much to win over new users. Gecko is now primarily used for the Mozilla derivatives such as Netscape and Mozilla Firefox.

Mozilla's evolution: from Mozilla Suite to Mozilla Firefox

Following the release of the source code, the Mozilla Project at first struggled to attract outside developers (Mockus et al., 2002). On March 31, 1999, one year after the release of the source code, Jamie Zawinski, one of the Mozilla project leaders, left the project, citing lack of outside interest because of the large size, cumbersome architecture, absence of a working product, and lack of adequate support from Netscape as reasons for his departure (Mockus et al., 2002; Zawinski, 1999).

In mid-2000, Mozilla had not yet garnered the massive development effort from outside Netscape that the Mozilla founders had originally hoped for. Eric Raymond commented:

> "The problem here seems to be that for a long time the Mozilla distribution actually broke one of the basic rules of the bazaar model; it didn't ship with something potential contributors could easily run and see working." And: "most negatively (from the point of view of the outside world) the Mozilla group didn't ship a production-quality browser for two and a half years after the project launch – and in 1999 one of the project's principals caused a bit of a sensation by resigning, complaining of poor management and missed opportunities. 'Open source,' he correctly observed, 'is not magic pixie dust.'"[5]

After a series of lengthy pre-1.0 release cycles, Mozilla 1.0, also called Mozilla Suite or Mozilla Application Suite, was finally released on June 5, 2002. Reactions to the new suite were mixed.

Before AOL spun it off, Mozilla had been positioning itself as the browser of choice for developers of mobile application software, and promised that Mozilla 1.0 would be modularized, consisting of small, easily separated components (*CNET News*, October 13, 2004). Instead, developers conceded after Mozilla 1.0's launch that the program had become "large and unwieldy" (*CNET News*, October 15, 2003). The suite was accused of trying to do too many things: being a web browser, an email program, an HTML editor and a chat program, and focusing too much on features (*Arstechnica*, November 9, 2004).

These concerns led to the creation of what became known as the Firefox project.[6] The project was initiated by Blake Ross, a longtime contributor to the Mozilla browser, and Dave Hyatt, an ex-Netscape employee with an intimate knowledge of the code, who were both disappointed with the direction of the Mozilla project. They believed that the commercial requirements of Netscape's sponsorship only made the browser more complex and harmed the utility and potential of the Mozilla browser (Redcouch, "Mozilla Firefox"). Ross and Hyatt therefore intended to develop a lightweight alternative to the heavy Mozilla suite.[7] In 2002, Ross and Hyatt announced they had started a "fork" out of the browser component of the Mozilla code base, combining Mozilla's layout engine Gecko, and using a new user interface language, XUL (McHugh, 2005). The need for a stand-alone and more agile browser became even more clear in January 2003 when the slow progress and size of the Mozilla Suite prompted Apple Computer to pass over Mozilla in favor of the KHTML[8] open source codebase for its Safari browser (*CNET News*, January 14, 2003).

By that time, the Firefox project had its own perils. Hyatt had accepted a job at Apple in late 2002, while Ross started to attend Stanford. After the departures of Hyatt and Ross the project seemed to stumble, but was carried on by Ben Goodger, under whose guidance a serviceable beta version of Firefox was released just before Summer 2003. However, by the beginning of 2004, the project had lost much of its credibility after chronic delays of the browser (Festa, P., *CNET News*, December, 2004). Firefox 1.0 was eventually released in November 2004 and received wide acclaim. The browser was praised in magazines (*Business Week*), newspapers (*Financial Times*, *Wall Street Journal*), websites (e.g., BBC.com), and received several awards. Market share rose to about 4.64% in December 2004 (NetApplications estimate).

In 2004, Nokia provided the Mozilla Foundation with funding to produce a cell-phone browser based on the Mozilla code base (*CNET News*, June 18, 2004). The resulting project, called "Minimo" (mini-Mozilla) released a preview version, Minimo 007, in July 2005.[9] With the release of Minimo 007 it was further stated that "Minimo plans within the next five to six months a 'beta' test version for use with Windows CE PPC and Windows CE SmartPhone" (*CNET News*, July 26, 2005).

To address developers' concerns about the size of the Mozilla Suite and to capitalize on Firefox's success, the Mozilla Foundation on March 10, 2005 officially announced that it would stop developing the Mozilla Suite so that developers could focus on Firefox and the email program Thunderbird.[10] The Mozilla suite was unofficially superseded by SeaMonkey, an Internet suite to be developed and released by the Mozilla community, based on the source code of the Mozilla Suite.

Mozilla Firefox 1.5, based on Gecko 1.8 and initially scheduled for release in September 2005, was released on November 29, 2005. Firefox 2.0, based on Gecko 1.8.1, was released in October 2006 and included improvements to Bookmarks/History and per-site options.[11] Firefox 3.0, to be based on Gecko 1.9, is planned for the first quarter of 2008 (Cabello, P., Mozillalinks, November 24, 2007).[12]

Mozilla (Firefox) development model[13]

As pointed out earlier, Mozilla.org was created to function as a *clearinghouse*, that is, an online meeting place for contributors where contributions are listed in a database. The site further functions as coordinator and facilitator for further development of the Mozilla codebase. The Mozilla.org website states that

> It can be observed that all successful open-source software projects follow this model of distributed development and centralized integration. One of the fears that open-source software neophytes often express is that open availability of the source will lead to balkanization, that there will eventually be thousands of different descendants of the original software, and confusion and chaos will result. But, in reality that doesn't happen; organizations like mozilla.org tend to appear. Eric Raymond tries to explain why in his excellent paper, The Cathedral and the Bazaar. We hope to

operate in the "Bazaar" style, and be to the public Netscape source code as Linus Torvalds is to Linux.[14]

One of Mozilla.org's most important roles is to decide which contributions (posted on Mozilla.org) warrant inclusion in the main distribution or branch of the Mozilla codebase (Hamerly et al., 1999). To enable effective development, the total Mozilla codebase is divided into modules, with each major code module having its own lead developer or "owner."[15] To "promote distributed decision making by the development community" Mozilla.org has delegated decision-making authority to the module owner (Baker, 2004: 1). This module owner, often a key contributor, knows the code best, reviews the contributions with the help of a few "peers," and decides what should go into the module and what not (Baker, 2004).[16] Following the inclusions of contributions to the module, the owner sends the changes to Mozilla.org for inclusion in the Foundation's code repository or database on which the Foundation's distribution/release will be based.[17]

During the development of the Mozilla Suite, getting a contribution "checked in" involved a review both from a module owner or peer and from a super-reviewer.[18] If the two reviewers approved the code, it would be likely to be included in the main distribution. The founders of the Firefox project blamed this cumbersome approach for Mozilla Suite getting "bloated," meaning increasing in size and complexity, and for causing an overall lack of strong direction.[19] Firefox was therefore different from the start.[20] The initial development team could approve contributions without any need for reviews, allowing the browser to develop quickly, especially in its early stages. Later on, contributions from other developers were accepted, with just one Firefox peer required to review each contribution before including it in the main codebase.[21] Consequently, at all points of the development of Firefox, a small group has had the privilege of checking in code (Krishnamurthy, 2005a).

Mozilla.org (and Firefox) operates as a meritocracy: "the more good code you develop, the more you will be allowed to contribute [...] the more responsibility you will be given."[22]

Firefox's style of "by invitation only" membership of the main development team that performs the most important tasks has been termed "closed-door projects" (Krishnamurthy, 2005a).[23] Users can provide feedback through forums but the actual development is done by a core group. This approach has drawn criticism from the OSS society, as it has been seen as discouraging outside contributions (Ross, 2005).

Firefox contributors

Although Gecko's modular architecture allows for development with a great number of programmers[24], the entire Firefox browser, as mentioned before, was mainly developed by a small team of committed programmers. In June 2005, six developers, Blake Ross, David Hyatt, Ben Goodger, Brian Ryner, Vladmir Vukicevic and Mike Conner, formed the Firefox core group (Krishnamurthy, 2005a). A significant part of this core group was paid a salary by the Mozilla Foundation to work on the Firefox project (Krishnamurthy, 2005a). Most Firefox lead developers are now paid by Mozilla Corp. or employed by one of Mozilla's partners (e.g., Google) and contribute to Firefox (to a lesser extent) from those positions.

Mozilla Firefox is developed by three "categories" of people: (1) employees of Mozilla Corp.; (2) employees of companies or institutions that contribute to the Mozilla project (e.g., Google); and (3) (unpaid) volunteers.[25] Firefox development and testing are mostly done by about a dozen Mozilla employees, plus a few dozen others at companies like IBM, Sun, and Red Hat.[26] By February 2005, Sun Microsystems already employed a dozen Firefox developers in Beijing, and IBM had two dozen Firefox developers in Austin, Texas (McHugh, 2005).

The exact importance and number of contributions by unpaid volunteers or contributors not related to an institution or company seems limited in significance, as, inherent to the structure of Mozilla. org, the most important contributions are being made by the lead team, consisting of "non-volunteers." Strong leadership has indeed been practiced in the Firefox project from the start, with the peers not afraid to reject contributions.[27] This might, together with the Firefox "meritocracy," have discouraged and alienated potential developers.

The Mozilla Foundation website states that the project has more than 800 code contributors[28] and thousands of testers, designers and writers worldwide.[29] According to Ben Goodger, Firefox's lead engineer: "hundreds of engineers have contributed code, hundreds and thousands more testing and other types of materials, probably millions of man-hours spent."[30] Goodger further stated that volunteers had made important contributions in the area of visual identity and the testing and reporting of bugs. As a comparison, in November 2004, Microsoft had a team of more than 100 full-time developers working on IE (Lohr and Markoff, 2004).

However, on March 3, 2005, Mike Connor, a Firefox core team developer, raised a red flag concerning the Firefox methodology of development. On his blog he complained:

> In nearly three years, we haven't built up a community of hackers around Firefox, for a myriad of reasons, and now I think we are in trouble. Of the six people who can actually review in Firefox, four are AWOL, and one doesn't do a lot of reviews. And I'm on the verge of just walking away indefinitely.[31]

He also criticized the staffing priorities of the Mozilla Foundation, which in his eyes did not do enough to support Firefox. He further questioned whether the Foundation had a plan. In an earlier post, he had already complained about the community involvement, noting that:

> seemingly, I'm the most responsive peer for Firefox reviews, which presents a problem for me. So I'm finding that I'm stuck between actually reviewing code, or making money. [...] Every hour I spend on Firefox instead of my contract work costs me money.[32]

He didn't blame his fellow core group developers though, "Ben just landed the massive prefwindow V changes, plus whatever he's really doing at Google. Blake's in school and starting a company. Vlad and Bryner are occupied by their employers' respective Mozilla priorities."[33]

In his next post, on March 11, 2005, Connor tuned down his previous disappointment and criticism, noting that, "I believe that we're making a lot of moves in the right direction now" and that "I have no intention of leaving or abandoning the project."[34]

The Mozilla Foundation's decision not long after that to officially abandon the Mozilla Suite, and instead focus on Firefox, not long after Connor's remarks, suggests that Mozilla heeded Connor's call.

Mozilla Firefox product/standard phase

Quality

Firefox has received wide praise from Internet experts for its features, which include site-specific pop-up blocking, live bookmarks, tabbed browsing, privacy options, and an extension mechanism for adding Google and other search tools built into the toolbar. Although other browsers have also introduced these features, Firefox became the first such browser to achieve wide adoption. The browser is further regarded as being more innovative than Microsoft's IE and less susceptible to malicious programs that routinely attack IE (Lohr and Markoff, 2004). In the summer of 2004, the United States Computer Emergency Readiness Team, a group overseen by the Department of Homeland Security, even suggested that computer users switch to browsers other than IE as one approach to reduce vulnerability to computer viruses. In particular IE's ActiveX controls, small parts of software that enhance a site's functionality, proved to be very vulnerable to abuse, for example, downloading spyware or adware on a user's PC. Other security features of Firefox are particularly geared towards "phishing," which misleads users into thinking that they are visiting a legitimate site while they are not. However, Firefox has had to issue patches to counter several serious security flaws[35] for Firefox 1.0 and for Firefox 1.5 in December 2005 (*CNET News*, December 8, 2005; *CNET News*, September 21, 2005). In September 2005, the security company Symantec even announced in a hotly contested report that more bugs had been found in Mozilla browsers than in IE in the first six months of 2005 (*CNET News*, September 19, 2005). As of January 12, 2006, IE 6.0, with all vendor patches installed and all vendor workarounds applied, still had 21 of the 92 security flaws identified by Secunia marked as unpatched, with several of the flaws rated "Highly critical."[36] Firefox scored much better, with only three out of the 26 identified security flaws marked as unpatched, none of the unaddressed flaws being critical.[37] Firefox has been prompt in releasing patches once vulnerability has been found. "Wired" (issue of February 2005)[38] attributed this rapid response to the open-source nature of the browser. Mozilla also established the Bug Bounty program on September 14, 2004, to reward contributors for discovering bugs and helping to continually improve Mozilla's products. Everybody who reports a security flaw receives a $500 cash reward.

Firefox 1.5, based on the Gecko 1.8 lay-out engine, improved its standards support, and provided some new options like "drag and drop" and supported new web standards such as AJAX, while enhancing its features. Firefox 1.5, furthermore, was the first browser to offer accessibility options for visually and/or physically disabled web surfers.[39]

Firefox has been awarded several prizes, for example, Product of the Year in PC World (2005); PC Magazine Editor's Choice in Sarrel, PC Mag.com (2005); CNET Editor's Choice (2004); and was recommended over IE by CNET Review: "Move over, Internet Explorer. Feature-studded and secure Mozilla Firefox 1.0 is a safer, better choice for Internet browsing" (*CNET News*, November 10, 2004); Rapoza, eWeek, (2004): "Firefox 1.0 Lives Up to Hype"; BBC News (2004): "Firefox browser takes on Microsoft"; Pegoraro, Washington Post (2004): "Firefox leaves no reason to endure Internet Explorer"; Mossberg, *Wall Street Journal* (2004): "Security, Cool Features Of Firefox Web Browser Beat Microsoft's IE." The browser is available for Windows 98, Windows 2000, Windows XP, Windows Vista, Mac OS X, and Linux, in contrast to IE, which only runs on Windows-based OSs (Mozilla.com Release Note 2.0.0.9).[40]

Price

Firefox is open source software, also meaning that, as its website points out, "anyone has the right to download and use the browser for free, to distribute it unmodified to other people, and even to view and modify the source code under the terms of the Mozilla Public License."[41] Firefox can also be bought on CD-ROM from the online Mozilla store.

The Mozilla Foundation has rejected the idea of becoming a support-oriented business, charging for help, as Red Hat does for Linux. According to Mitchell Baker, President of the Mozilla Foundation: "we are a nonprofit organization, so our goal is diversity on the Web and maintaining a Web that isn't controlled by a small number of vendors. We need to generate enough money to sustain ourselves. So in that sense we are not like the for-profit Linux support provider Red Hat." (*CNET News*, October 15, 2003). With the creation of Mozilla Corp., Mozilla reaffirmed that "Firefox and Thunderbird will remain as they are today: free of charge products based on open source code."[42]

License

Following the announcement that it would release its source code, the Netscape release team had extensively reviewed existing OSS licenses to see whether these would be appropriate for Netscape's source code release. However, existing licenses were insufficiently fit to balance the goal of engaging OSS developers while protecting Netscape's business interests. The company therefore decided to create a new license: the Netscape Public License (NPL). The NPL was similar to the GNU General Public License (LGPL)[43] but would allow Netscape to continue to publish proprietary versions of its browser, containing publicly released or contributed code. Its most controversial feature was that the NPL gave Netscape the right to distribute/relicense code contributed by others to third parties, under terms different from the NPL, including commercial terms, without granting similar rights to those contributors (Hamerley et al., 1999). This "asymmetry in rights" was heavily criticized by the open source community.

In reaction, the firm announced the Mozilla Public License (MPL).[44] The Mozilla Public License is similar to the NPL but lacks the asymmetry in rights. Under the MPL, Netscape cannot regain proprietary rights to modifications of the source code. In fact, the terms of the MPL are even stricter than those of the GPL (Lerner and Tirole, 2004).

Development of Mozilla-based proprietary products is also made easier by the terms of the Mozilla Public License (MPL), which, unlike other more restrictive open source licenses, does not require developers to turn their Mozilla-based applications back over to the open source effort. It is therefore possible to use Mozilla code to create a product, or to combine Mozilla code with other code to create that product (Baker, 2004). The latter is exactly what Netscape did with Netscape 6.0, 7.0 and 8.0, and plans to do in the future.[45] Based on the most recent Mozilla code, the company added a set of Netscape-specific items and additional code to create its Netscape 6. Other parties are free to use a part of the Mozilla code (e.g., the Gecko layout engine) in a product (Baker, 2004).

All of the Communicator 4.0 source code initially issued on March 31, 1998 was released under the NPL, which stipulated that all modifications to that code must also be released under the NPL. New code could, however, be released under the MPL (Hamerly et al., 1999).[46]

In 2001, Mozilla announced a relicensing effort, to get all mozilla. org-hosted code licensed under an MPL/GPL/LGPL tri-license in order to address concerns about potential incompatibilities between the MPL and the GPL and LGPL.[47] This relicensing enabled Mozilla contributors and developers building products based on Mozilla to choose whether to use the code under the terms of the MPL, the GPL or the LGPL.[48] In January 2004, Mozilla announced that in the following months the majority of the Mozilla codebase including Firefox would be relicensed under the MPL/GPL/LGPL tri-license.[49] Time Warner, which now owns Netscape, has, at the request of the Mozilla Foundation and exercising its rights under the NPL, relicensed all code in Mozilla that was under the NPL to the MPL/GPL/LGPL tri-license, thus effectively removing the GPL-incompatibility.[50]

Complementary products

One of the most powerful features of Firefox is the many hundreds of extras, or extensions, produced for it. The open source nature of the program allows for the creation of add-ons or extensions by individual developers. The add-ons initially raised security concerns. To address these concerns, the Mozilla Foundation opened Mozilla Update, a site containing extensions "approved" by Mozilla.org.[51] An example of a popular extension is ForecastFox, which displays live weather information on the status bar.[52] At the time of the release of Firefox 1.5, developers had already created more than 700 extensions (*CRN*, August 9, 2005).[53] Add-ons include search toolbars for Google, Amazon and Yahoo.[54]

Extensions are also offered for IE, but on a much smaller basis compared with Firefox. IE's most popular extension is the Google toolbar.

Compatibility and standards

IE is exclusively linked to Microsoft's operating system Windows, but Firefox can be also used in combination with Mac OS X, Linux, BSD and Unix. Users of these operation systems have to find an alternative to IE, and then Firefox turns out to be their favorite choice.

In the early 2000s, many sites were designed with WYSIWYG HTML programs such as Macromedia Dreamweaver or Microsoft FrontPage. These programs often generated non-standard HTML by default, hindering the work of the W3C in developing standards.

Internet standards were allegedly further weakened by Microsoft dominating the web browser industry.[55] Many web developers wrote their websites to work with IE's idiosyncrasies, rather than sticking to the standards. Although at the time of its launch IE 6.0 was widely praised for its standard compliance, the browser has in recent years been criticized as outdated, failing to keep pace with browser standards, and lacking support for basic standards such as CSS (Taylor (2004), and *CNET News*, October 9, 2003). Microsoft showed an unwillingness to adhere to standards by introducing new, proprietary extensions such as VBScript and Active X (Microsoft, "Chapter Two"[56]: Inside Microsoft Visual Basic Scripting Edition). In 2003, Microsoft announced that IE 6.0 (SP1) would be the last stand-alone version of its browser, and the browser would be part of the evolution of its Windows platform Windows Vista. The new operating system was to include XAML, a proprietary XML language, to allow for the development of elaborate web applications, and hoped to make stand-alone browsers obsolete by incorporating web browsing into the desktop (McHugh, 2005).[57] This move would basically give Microsoft control over the Internet's *de facto* standards (McHugh, 2005). In response, probably worried by what consequences this might have for its comparable XUL[58], the Mozilla Foundation on April 2004 joined efforts with Opera Software to develop new open standards which would add more capabilities while remaining backwards compatible with the existing technologies. The collaboration was formalized in the Web Hypertext Application Technology Working Group (WHATWG)[59] and was also joined by Apple.

Microsoft surprised web standard advocates in July 2005 when it entered into a partnership with the Web Standards Project (WaSP), a web standard advocacy group, to help Microsoft products adhere to standards. Following the collaboration, Microsoft appeared to be moving towards acceptance of browser standards, proposed by W3C (*CNET News*, August 4, 2005).

The Mozilla Foundation has since stated that its goal is "to promote innovation on the Web and to help keep the Internet *open* [...] by developing open source Internet client software, designed to comply with *open standards*, to be cross-platform, and to be internationalization-ready. The result is an award-winning suite of products [...] that are widely renowned for their *excellent standards support*."[60] When Firefox 1.0 was launched, Brendan Eich, a former Netscape engineer who is now the chief software architect of the Mozilla Foundation, commented "this is really about taking back the Web and not having to rely on the technology and technology standards of one company" (Lohr and Markoff, 2004).

Firefox is acknowledged to have good support for existing standards, particularly those of the W3C, which, if followed by the web designer, ensures a correct display regardless of the browser.[61] Firefox 1.5 featured improved support for CSS2 and CSS3, as well as many DHTML, JavaScript, and DOM enhancements.[62] As of 2005 there is strong competition between Mozilla's Gecko layout engine, Opera's Presto layout engine, and the KHTML engine used in Apple's Safari browser, with each of them leading in terms of different aspects of CSS. IE remains the worst at translating CSS standards (MSDN Internet Explorer Blog, 2006).[63]

In December 2007, the Norwegian software maker Opera submitted a complaint to the European Commission about misuse by Microsoft of its dominant position in the market. Opera accuses Microsoft of not implementing open standards that prescribe how web pages should be shown in browsers. Therefore, many website designers have adapted their sites for use with IE, which causes problems if the sites are viewed using other browsers. Opera asks the European Commission to force Microsoft to correctly implement the standards. Opera also asks the European Commission to force Microsoft to clearly separate IE from Windows or to also provide other browsers preinstalled with Windows.[64]

Availability of support

Users can obtain support for Mozilla Firefox in many ways. Free support is provided by online documentation on Firefox's support site www.mozilla.org/support/firefox and by the Mozilla community on the support forums, newsgroups and online chat sites. Recently, the first books with tips about the browser have emerged (e.g., McFarlene N., "Firefox Hacks" (2005)). Paid telephone support by a third-party provider was first introduced in October 2003 with the release of Mozilla 1.5 (*CNET News*, October 15, 2003). Mozilla-based products are further offered (and thus supported) by third parties such as IBM and the MozDev Group.

Table 7.2 provides an overview of Firefox's relevant Product/Standard characteristics.

Table 7.2 Overview of product/standard characteristics of Mozilla Firefox

Characteristics	Mozilla Firefox
General	
Creator	Mozilla Foundation
Layout engine	Gecko
Release version	2.0 (November 24, 2006)
Quality	
Security	Security enhancements within Firefox 2 continue. New is a dialog box informing of cross-domain scripting, a tactic used by criminal hackers to link nonrelated sites to sites which may be perceived as legitimate. And Mozilla remains very responsive to fixing its vulnerabilities, pushing out updates within a few days of public notice. Microsoft, on the other hand, parses out its vulnerability fixes a little at a time. In the 5 years since its release, IE 6 has accrued a large deficit, and there is no sign that Microsoft is addressing new vulnerabilities found in IE 7 any faster.
Features	Bookmark managing; Download managing; Password managing; Form managing; Search engine toolbar; Tabbed browsing; Pop-up blocking; Incremental finding; Antiphishing technology.
Operating system support	Windows; Mac OS X; Linux; BSD; Unix
Price	Free
License	
Software license	MPL, MPL/GPL/LGPL tri-license (source code can be modified, allows for combination with proprietary software and non-free derivatives)
Standards support	CSS2; Frames; Java; JavaScript; XSLT; XHTML; MathML; Xforms; RSS; Atom; XPath. Firefox 2 does not fully support all the standards supported by the W3C organization, so it fails what is called the Acid2 test, a test designed by the Web Standards Project, although Mozilla is working hard toward full compliance. For comparison, of the browsers tested by CNET, only Opera 9 passed the test; IE 7 fared the worst, unable to translate the page in the correct colors or shapes.

Continued

Table 7.2   Continued

Characteristics	Mozilla Firefox
Compatibility	
Between versions	The underlying Web rendering engine within Firefox 2 is Gecko 1.8, and it is largely unchanged from the previous release, Firefox 1.5. The next release of Firefox should include a new rendering engine.
With other browsers	Incompatible with ActiveX or other Internet Explorer-specific code (so some websites might not display properly).
Availability of complements	Many extensions.
Availability of support	Through third parties, extensive manuals are available online.

Source: Based on Vamosi, R., PC Mag.com, "Review Firefox 2.0," http://reviews.cnet.com/browsers/firefox-2/4505–3514_7-32126746.html?tag=pm, last accessed January 8, 2008.

Mozilla Firefox acceptance phase

Firefox's entry and rise to popularity

In 2003, Microsoft had announced that IE would no longer be made available as a separate product, but that it would be part of the evolution of its Windows platform and that the browser would only be upgraded when installing new versions of its operating system. This basically meant that users of any existing Microsoft operating system would never be able to obtain an upgrade for their IE browser on their current systems as their PCs were not powerful enough to run Windows XP.[65] As IE 6.0 (SP 2) security enhancements were only available to those who were using XP, which costs $99 to upgrade to, consumers using old Windows operating systems such as ME or 98 were increasingly vulnerable to attacks on their PCs.

Because Microsoft halted innovation of its IE browser and because of security concerns about the IE, some Web surfers were prompted to seek alternatives. Firefox increasingly became a credible substitute for IE, offering new features and enhanced security.

In the five months preceding the release of Firefox 1.0, an estimated eight million people downloaded preview versions of the browser (Lohr and Markoff, 2004).

On November 9, 2004 Mozilla Firefox 1.0 was officially released. The browser became an instant hit, with 25 million downloads in the 99 days after its release. At that time, the browser held a market share of about 6.17% (NetApplications estimate). The release of Firefox 1.0 was accompanied by a community-led marketing campaign, the Spread Firefox Campaign.[66] On September 12, 2004, the "Spread Firefox portal" (www.spreadfirefox.com) was opened. The site offered suggestions on how to best market Firefox, discussed marketing techniques, facilitated marketing events and honored the most effective Firefox "marketers." The site further boasted referral buttons to be placed on websites with slogans like "Rediscover the web" and "The browser you can trust," not too subtly aiming at IE. As of November 26, 2007, more than 682,000 websites were linked to the Firefox page, with an additional 183,000 linking to mozilla.org.[67] To help spread the release of Firefox, the Spread Firefox Campaign asked users to donate $10 towards a full-page advertisement on Firefox in the *New York Times*. Over 10,000 people together donated the needed sum of $250,000 in less than 48 hours, and the advert ran in the *New York Times* of December 15, 2004. Other sites, like www.switch2firefox.com, were opened to persuade users to trade IE for Firefox (Krishnamurthy, 2005b). Much marketing work is done by the community voluntarily free of charge. On November 26, 2007, the Mozilla Foundation's full-time staff consisted of not more then 17 people[68]. To further Mozilla's cause, the Foundation also established affiliates in Europe, Japan and China.[69]

In 2005, the Mozilla Foundation created Mozilla Corp. to handle the revenue-related operations of Mozilla.[70] The press release that accompanied the announcement of the creation of Mozilla Corp. offered a clue as to what inspired this move:

> The broad adoption of Mozilla Firefox has created significant economic value both in Firefox itself and in a commercial ecosystem that is developing around Firefox. This economic value is an unintended but real by-product of the Mozilla project's overriding goal of providing a Web browser with enough market-share to drive open standards on the Web. Carefully managed, this value – and

the resulting ability to generate revenue – can be used to make the Mozilla project self-sustaining and help keep the Internet open and diverse.

The wholly owned subsidiary of the Mozilla Foundation is responsible for product development, marketing (including the management of relationship with partners), and distribution of Mozilla products.[71] Following the creation of Mozilla Corp., the Mozilla Foundation has limited its focus to policy issues, and project governance and promotion of other Mozilla open source projects, such as SeaMonkey. It further maintains control of the Mozilla source code, and the Mozilla trademarks and intellectual property, which it licenses to the Mozilla Corporation.

Most of the Mozilla Foundation employees have been transferred to the new organization. At the time of creation, Mozilla Corp. employed about 30 people, and the Mozilla Foundation about three. On September 11, 2007, Firefox reached a new milestone, achieving its 400 millionth download. On November 2, Firefox 2.0.0.9 was released on the Mozilla website (www.mozilla.com). At that time, Firefox's market share was estimated at 17.4 %.[72]

The release of Firefox 1.5 was again accompanied by a marketing campaign. The centerpiece of the new marketing blitz consisted of user-submitted videos of Firefox users advocating their favorite web browser (called Flicks), made available at the SpreadFirefox website.[73]

The Mozilla Foundation had reportedly been talking to OEMs to get Firefox installed on PCs by default instead of IE, which is, together with other Microsoft software, preloaded on most PCs (*CNET News,* November 9, 2004). In December 2005, Mozilla had its first success when Dell announced that it was to start launching the Firefox browser preinstalled on its PCs.[74] This is still being preinstalled, mostly next to the already existing IE browsers which come along with the Windows operating system.[75]

Microsoft's reaction

When asked about Firefox threatening Microsoft's business, Steve Vamos, head of Microsoft's Australian operations, stated in November 2004 that he did not believe that the threat posed by Firefox was real, and that "there is a lot of hype surrounding the open source movement" (*ZDNET* Australia, November 11, 2004). Bill Gates commented on Firefox in a rather condescending manner, noting that "so much software gets downloaded all the time, but do people actually use it?" (BBC News, May 9, 2005).

In May 2007, Microsoft announced the development of Internet Explorer 8.0 as the next step after the deployment of Internet Explorer 7.0 in Windows XP, Windows 2003 Server and Windows Vista. The 8.0 browser is being developed, mainly across layout, object model and Ajax development fronts. The design is intended to be more compliant with the CSS 2.1 layout standard and to be more interoperable with that used by other browsers. Furthermore, it should provide more client-side application programming interfaces (APIs) to support local storage for mash-ups.[76]

Microsoft's decision to bring forward the new version of IE can be interpreted as a move to counter the rising popularity of Firefox and the subsequent decrease in IE's market share (Morisson and Waters, 2005). According to MicrosoftWatch.com, a website that monitors and analyzes Microsoft, the decision to refresh IE came after some major Microsoft customers threatened to move to Firefox if Microsoft failed to do so.[77]

When Microsoft launched Live.com, its service aimed at bringing a number of business services closely aligned with Microsoft Office products to users over the Internet[78], in November 2005, the company added support for Firefox (PCPRO.co.uk, November 10, 2005). By making this decision, Microsoft indirectly admitted that Firefox had sufficient market share to warrant such support.

Third party support

Mozilla Corp. can count on a number of allies for support: many of them are Microsoft rivals. Partners include IBM, Google, Sun Microsystems, Hewlett Packard, Oracle, Red Hat, Novell, and Lindows.[79] The direct need for support of Mozilla by third parties was prompted when Netscape halted the development of Mozilla in July 2003. The companies had varying reasons for this support.

Unix systems vendors such as IBM, HP and Sun were left without a browser that supported their system. Without this browser they would not be able to sell their Internet-connected work stations. The companies therefore each assigned some of their own engineers to the Mozilla Project, to ensure its continuance and to guarantee that new releases of the Mozilla browser would be compatible with their systems (West and Gallagher, 2005).

Some software vendors such as IBM also use the Mozilla platform, the Mozilla browser, the source code, or Mozilla development tools to create proprietary applications and other products.[80] IBM adopted a multi-browser strategy in spring 2005 after about 10% of its employees downloaded Firefox (Morisson and Waters, 2005). Big Blue also encouraged its employees to use Firefox as their default browser (*CNET News*, May 12, 2005). IBM has further updated its Workplace desktop software for Linux with support for Firefox (*CNET News*, August 9, 2005). Another reason for IBM to support Mozilla is that Firefox also runs on the Linux OS in which IBM has an interest. The latter reason for support applies to Red Hat as well.

Google's motivation to collaborate with Mozilla Corp. and contribute to Firefox is thought to be that such cooperation allows Microsoft's online archrival to improve its products and reach new users, which reduces Google's dependence on the browser of rival Microsoft, which, moreover, offers the competing search engine Microsoft Search (Morisson and Waters, 2005).

Support for Mozilla by third parties mostly includes contributions by the companies' engineers.

Aside from a Nokia donation to the Minimo project to develop a cell phone browser, no major direct cash donations seem to have been made. Two key Firefox backers are IBM and Google. For the development of Firefox 1.5, IBM donated DHTML accessibility code currently going through the W3C's standards process.[81] The code is important for XML, and AJAX, which is to power the Web 2.0 applications, and will allow Firefox to enhance "accessibility functions for visual- and motor-impaired Web surfers."[82]

Google has been working closely with Mozilla Corp. on the development of Firefox, employing several key Firefox developers (Morisson and Waters, 2005). Following an agreement reached in 2004, Firefox had already included Google as the default option for users wanting to search the Web via the Firefox searching box and since July 2005 also via a toolbar included in Firefox, which allows users to select the desired engine (*CNET News*, November 11, 2004). With the release of Firefox 1.5 in November 2005, Firefox also offered access to the Yahoo search engine. Mozilla has further partnerships with Yahoo, AskJeeves and online vendors such as Amazon and EBay.

Revenues from these contracts constitute by far the most important and significant income source for Mozilla (*Softpedia News*, 2005). According to Mozilla Foundation, the contracts with these companies generate a few million dollars on an annual basis (*Forbes*, August 3, 2005). Google has further agreed to host the Firefox default start page (www.google.com/firefox), which features a Google search entry, on its servers, and has hosted a Mozilla developer conference (McHugh, 2005). On January 6, 2006, Google announced Google Pack, a bundle of freely downloadable software. Besides Google's own software, the package includes third party software such as Mozilla Firefox.[83] Recent developments show that the relationship between Google and Firefox has been intensified: "The Google Anti-Phishing relationship will be expanded in Firefox 3.0. While Google currently is the default provider of a blacklist of known phishing sites to the browser, this will be enhanced to include a blacklist of sites that serve up malicious software" (Soghoian, CNET.com, November 1, 2007).[84] Google being implemented in Firefox is, for Firefox, an advantage it might not be willing to give up in the event of the relationship ending. Most of Firefox's users indicate that they like the Google search experience. Recently, Google introduced its own free gOS operating system[85], which is fully designed around the Google services.[86] In this operating system, Firefox is a standard application for accessing the web.

Competition from other browsers

Competition for Firefox is not limited to IE. The browser further faces competition from alternatives such as Opera and Safari.

Like Firefox, the non-open source browser Opera includes innovative features such as pop-up blocking, tabbed browsing, and integrated searching. The company first charged $39 for an ad-free version. However, after the release of Firefox, Opera's sales went down dramatically (*CNET News*, November 26, 2005). Opera therefore decided that with the release of Opera 8.5 on September 20, 2005, the browser would be available free of charge and without advertisements (although the company still sells support contracts) (Bray, 2005). Opera has further stated that its goal is to replace Firefox as the second most-used web browser (Bray, 2005), but its market share remains limited. In 2006, Opera started to expand its activities on the mobile market and the gaming market. Recently Firefox also started developing its own mobile browser (Shankland, October 10, 2007).[87]

Safari is Apple's web browser. It claims to be the fastest browser on any platform, loading up pages two times faster than IE 7 and 1.7 times faster than Firefox 2.0.[88] Of course, Safari can be used in combination with Apple's Mac OS X. It can also be used on Windows but this is reported to cause some problems (Paul, 2007).

As for Netscape, little had been accomplished since it laid off or reassigned most of its employees in 2003, though it maintained its Netscape browser unit. AOL continued to release Netscape browsers, based on Mozilla, but these were reportedly developed by third party contractors and improvements were minimal, causing the browser's market share to fall to about 1–2%.

In August 2004, Netscape 7.2 was released, based on Mozilla 1.7.2. Mercury Communications was contracted to develop Netscape Browser 8.0 (ZDNet News, November 30, 2004). Netscape Browser 8.0, heavily focused on security, specifically on spyware and spoofing, was released on May 19, 2005. The browser was intended to challenge Firefox and IE, adding a new dimension to this browser war, which ironically, and after all, finds its origin in Netscape releasing its browser's source code. In June 2006, Netscape replaced its traditional portal home page with a design that should be more attractive to users, including interactive elements.[89] The future Netscape 9.0 will continue to do so, using the Firefox source code (Barylick, Powerpage,org, November 2, 2007).[90] It includes some new features, such as URL correction. Netscape 9.0 is available for Linux, Mac OS X and Windows. Meanwhile, Netscape's market share is negligible, except according to the figures provided by Janco Associates' IT Productivity Center (2008), who claim a market share in April 2008 of 9.68%. However, they also mention that installing Netscape 8.0 causes difficulties and in terms of market acceptance Netscape 8.0 has been a flop. The majority of Netscape users still use version 4.x. They expect that Netscape will lose most of its market share once people begin to upgrade Vista and newer computers with other browsers installed.

IT productivity Center (2008) mentions a rapidly increasing market share for Google Desktop, 4.01% in April 2008, whereas other sources do not mention market shares for this new browser. One of the strengths they mention is the integration of Google Desktop into the Internet for mobile computing.

Firefox's adopters and reasons for adoption

Firefox's growth in the early stages was primarily fueled by non-corporate, technologically advanced users (Perez, 2005).[91] The adoption seemed to be primarily driven by old IE and Netscape users, and increases in Firefox market share come primarily at the expense of IE. It is not clear to what extent new Internet users adopt Firefox.

The browser is now moving into the consumer mass market, but most large companies still stick with IE because they do not want to support two or more browsers (*Financial Times*, September 21, 2005), and most corporate IT departments are cautious when it comes to change (Taylor, 2005). A few large corporations have broadly adopted Firefox, for example, IBM. Some large companies are experimenting with the open source browser. Throughout 2005, Boeing has been providing feedback to the Mozilla Foundation on features that might encourage enterprise adoption of the browser (Sliwa, 2006). The company also made Firefox one of its corporate web browser standards (along with IE and Netscape). Fidelity Investments is another company that has been working with Mozilla on exploring the enterprise readiness of Firefox, but these companies are exceptions (Sliwa, 2006). In an email poll by Computerworld in the last 2 months of 2005, 86% of the 105 IT managers who responded indicated that IE was the sole browser at their company (Sliwa, 2006). Seven indicated that their company had a multi-browser or non-Microsoft standard. The poll further showed that 45% of the respondents used Firefox as their only browser or in addition to another browser, 21% indicated that their IT departments had added support for Firefox, and 70% said that Firefox had a positive effect on the IT industry. Some companies indicated that Firefox would be their preferred browser but that they are locked in by their reliance on applications that only function with IE (Sliwa, 2004).[92]

Several governmental organizations, such as the French Police (70,000 desktops), have also switched to Firefox (Noon, 2006). Companies that use Firefox are often reluctant to make public that they have migrated from IE to Firefox, as they are concerned that this may damage their relationship with Microsoft (Marson, 2005).

Gartner analyst Valdes also stressed the importance of broadening Firefox's user base by appealing to users other than Firefox early adopters to keep the momentum going: "Places to find new adopters are in the massive consumer market and in the corporate market, they say. One could argue they're getting close to saturating that portion of the market of technically adept users." However, Mozilla officials have acknowledged that, at least in the short term, their focus remains on individual users, not on making the browser attractive for IT departments that may in turn roll it out to their corporate users (Perez, 2005). Mike Shaver, a technology strategist at Mozilla Corp., explains why: "Mozilla typically focuses on consumer features, figuring that partners such as IBM, Novell and Red Hat are its 'best route to enterprise success' because they're more attuned to corporate needs" (Sliwa, 2006).

Firefox adoption appears to be stronger in Europe than in the United States.[93] In Europe, adoption seems to be driven by both consumers and governments, most likely due to the more positive attitude towards OSS in general.

The most important selling point of Firefox for both consumers and corporations is that it is perceived as more secure than IE, whose reputation has been tarnished by multiple hacker and virus attacks (Morrison, 2004; Broersma, 2005a). Another reason for adoption is that Firefox has more features, for example fidelity, can be customized, is more open standards-compliant, therefore less vendor-dependent,[94] and is more innovative (*Financial Times*, September 21, 2005), thus providing a better user experience (Broersma, 2005b).

Niche markets for Firefox are found in low-budget laptops and the third world, where low-budget laptops are being offered to the local and poor community. These laptops can be offered at a low price, mainly because the laptops come with open source software and an operating system, for example with gOS.[95] For Firefox this means a further expansion of its browser in this market, as the browser is delivered with every laptop being delivered.[96]

Furthermore, Firefox is about to enter the mobile browsers market , which is currently dominated by Opera Software ASA's Opera Mini, related to Apple.[97] This also means that the browser will be available on the Microsoft Windows Mobile operating system, and might go through the same process as happened in the market for desktop computers.[98]

Evaluation and summary of the characteristics of Firefox in Browser War II

OSS characteristics

Figure 7.1 provides an evaluation and explanation of the OSS characteristics of Firefox at the end of January 2006, when it had an estimated market share of about 10%. Firefox's position on the continuum is indicated by its logo.

OSS origin: The roots[99] of Firefox are predominantly "proprietary based": the main part of the codebase, the newly developed Gecko layout engine, was initially developed by Netscape. Further development of the codebase was undertaken by the "open" Mozilla community.

Development sponsorship: The initial development of Firefox was carried out by volunteers who were unhappy with the Mozilla Suite. Almost all of Firefox's main developers are now employed by firms such as Google and IBM, and continue to contribute to Firefox from this position. One can even argue that it has been this sponsorship that has helped Firefox move forward. Most key Firefox developers employed by firms are also module owners. Development sponsorship in terms of contribution is therefore heavily company sponsored.

The coordination is carried out under the responsibility of the independent Mozilla Foundation. Although the module owners can decide which code they want to include, the Foundation has the ultimate say. Given the existence of a Foundation assuming a facilitating and coordination role, and its ultimate decision-making authority, the development sponsorship in terms of coordination can be characterized as strongly leaning towards community sponsorship.

OSS program openness: Firefox is an OSS program in the sense that the source code is available and can be modified. Because the Firefox code can be combined with a non-OSS program and can be used to create a proprietary derivative, the program can be characterized as an OSS program with a proprietary (closed) leaning.

OSS program's compatibility: Firefox is completely compatible between different versions. Although the browser can appropriately display most of the websites specifically designed for IE, some do not translate properly, or do not translate at all. The compatibility with other programs is therefore not complete.

Price of OSS program: Firefox is a free web browser.

Availability of support for OSS program: Support is available for the browser (online forums, guidelines, and telephone support), although there seems to be less support available than for IE.

Quality of OSS program: The quality (made up of security, features and reliability) of Firefox is high when compared with alternative browsers.

Promotion sponsorship: The promotion sponsorship of Firefox can be characterized as being about midway between the two extremes of complete community sponsoring, that is, no direct promotion, and promotion only by a commercial firm, like Red Hat promoting Linux. The product is officially sponsored by the community, the Mozilla Foundation, a community platform which has become more institutionalized with the creation of Mozilla Corp., but is also promoted by commercial firms like Google, whose banner program includes Firefox in Google Pack, and IBM, which includes Firefox in its package and encourages employees to use Firefox. The program is also promoted by the OSS volunteer community at large via the SpreadFirefox campaign, for example, banners on websites, an approach which has been termed "community-led marketing" (Krishnamurthy, 2005b).

Strategic option: We will now briefly evaluate which of the three strategic options to compete identified by Hax and Wilde (1999) best describes the approach by which Firefox's sponsors compete.

At first sight, "System Lock-in" does not seem to be of much relevance, because this strategic option is based on creating a proprietary standard and locking-in the installed user base, which Firefox is not capable of due to its open nature. Moreover, migrating to another browser requires hardly any switching costs, and using two browsers next to each other is also an option. However, in another sense, System Lock-in applies: users with other operating systems than Windows have to look for another browser than IE. In this case, Firefox is the dominant alternative.

It seems that the Firefox's main sponsor, the Mozilla Foundation, competes on "differentiation": although a web browser is still a web browser, Firefox has, according to adopters and reviews, differentiated itself on security and features. The Mozilla Foundation, which by its own admission focuses on promoting Firefox to general users, tries to persuade these users by positioning and differentiating Firefox as being of superior product quality relative to IE. Hax's (2002: 5) description of Best Product as an approach to "attract, satisfy and retain the customer through the inherent characteristics of the product" fittingly explains the manner in which the Mozilla Foundation aims to further the adoption of the browser.

With regard to the commercial firms sponsoring Firefox by including the browser in their overall package, such as IBM, or sponsoring the browser in another way, for example, Google with Google Pack, identifying a univocal, clear strategic option is more complicated. One can, however, argue that these firms' promotion of Firefox can be explained by the Total Customer Solution option, where firms compete by "offering in cooperation with partners a broad bundle of products and services that is targeted and customized to a specific customer's needs" (Hax and Wilde, 1999: 13).

Three characteristics of Total Customer Solution (TCS) particularly explain how Firefox assists the approach sponsors like IBM compete through TCS:

1. Firefox is part of a total solution that consists of a set of products. The focus is not on the individual browser but on the set of products of which the browser is a part. Companies such as IBM offer adaptations of Firefox as a component of their suites. The open source nature of Firefox also allows it to be used as the basis for an open standards platform to which other software programs can tie in. Companies can also promote Firefox because Firefox allows these firms to also improve the quality of their complete product offerings, such as the Gmail and Google Earth services of Google, and makes the companies and customers less vendor-dependent because the browser is OSS.

2. A TCS is "based on *a wider offering* of products and services" (Hax and Wilde, 1999: p. 13). By incorporating Firefox into the company's solution, the company expands its product offering options. Proprietary elements can be added to the browser and it can be

Table 7.3   Standards-setting attributes: collaboration – competition

	Development phase	Product/standard phase	Acceptance Phase
Mode of standard selection	–	–	Market mode (Competition)
Effort to standardize	Joint (Collaboration)	Joint (Collaboration)	Joint (Collaboration)
Access to standard	Open (Collaboration)	Open (Collaboration)	–

combined with other OSS and proprietary software of the company, thus even further expanding the options which a complete package to the customer can offer. Incorporating Firefox in its total solution can therefore also be regarded as an extension of the company's competitive toolset.

3. When competing through TCS, a company "provides a portfolio of customized products and services that represent a unique value proposition to individualized customers" (Hax, 2002: 7). The open nature of Firefox particularly allows for such a customized solution to individual needs: even a proprietary derivative is possible.

Figure 7.1 summarizes the OSS characteristics of Firefox.

Standards-setting characteristics

We will now evaluate the standards-setting attributes of Osrhi and Weeber (2006) and the openness of Krechmer (2006), in all three phases, and the presence of standard war-related issues (two tactics and seven key assets) and standardization mechanisms in the acceptance phase, in the case of Firefox. Table 7.3 summarizes a characterization of the attributes of the different phases. Each of the attributes is characterized as leaning towards collaboration or competition. We will now provide a short explanation of the evaluation of the attributes.

Mode of standard selection: This attribute can be characterized as "market mode": the market decides which web browser will become the dominant one; IE, Firefox or another browser. This attribute is thus competitive in nature.

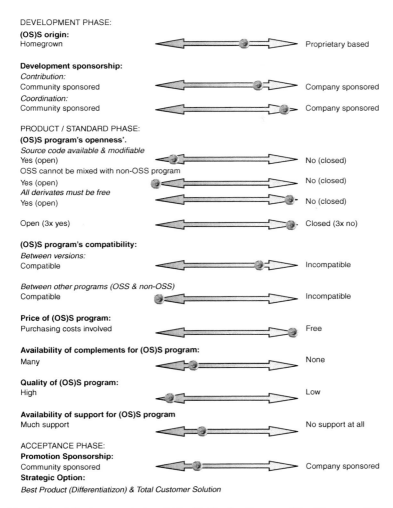

Figure 7.1 OSS characteristics of Mozilla Firefox (Browser War II): competition versus cooperation (January 2006, version 1.5)

Note: ● Firefox (until January 2006)

Effort to standardize: This attribute has a joint mode for all three phases: in the development phases developers from Mozilla Corp., employees from firms (also from rival standards-setters such as AOL/ Netscape), and volunteers all work together to develop the program.

Mozilla Corp. engages in collaboration with a rival when it joins efforts with Opera and Apple Safari to form the WHATWG group to develop open standards together. Finally, it collaborates in the acceptance phase with third party firms such as Google and IBM to spread Firefox. In both the development and the promotion, this collaboration is *not* formalized in a consortium.

Access to standard: Firefox is open in terms of future development as well as license. Most standards-setting attributes are collaborative in nature, which is not that surprising given the open nature of Firefox. We will now examine to what extent Krechmer's openness requirements, as outlined in the theoretical framework, are present in Browser War II. See also Table 7.4.

Table 7.4   Openness in different phases

	Requirement	Meaning of Requirement	Development	Product/ standard	Acceptance
			Phases		
1	Open meeting	All may participate in the standards development process	Yes, to some extent, but not in decision-making		
2	Consensus	All interests are discussed and agreement found, no domination	No		
3	Due process	Balloting and an appeals process may be used to find resolution	To some extent		
4	Open World	Same standard for the same capability, world-wide	Yes	Yes	Yes
5	Open IPR	How holders of IPR contained in the standard make available their IPR	Yes	Yes	Yes
6	Open change	All changes to existing standards are presented and agreed in a forum supporting the five requirements above	To some extent	Yes	Yes

Continued

Table 7.4 Continued

		Phases			
	Requirement	Meaning of Requirement	Development	Product/ standard	Acceptance
7	Open documents	Committee documents and completed standards are readily available		Yes	Yes
8	Open interface	Enables compatibility (backward and forward)		Yes	Yes
9	Open use	Relates to the assurances a user requires to use an implementation		Yes	Yes
10	Ongoing support	Standards should be supported until user interest ceases rather than when implementer interest declines			Yes

Source: Adapted from Krechmer (2006).

1. The Open Meeting requirement is fulfilled to some extent because everybody may contribute to the development of Firefox. However, not all contributors have the same responsibility and authority: Mozilla operates as a "meritocracy," in which membership of the key development team is "by invitation only." It therefore appears that, although there is an "open meeting" in the development, this process is not completely open, and decision-making is done by the core team only.

2. Consensus in the development does not seem to be a primary issue: the whole origin of Firefox lies in the fact that the creators were not content with the Mozilla Suite. Moreover, the module owners and Mozilla Foundation have the final say in what code gets accepted.

3. There appears to be a certain form of due process: contributions are reviewed by the Module owners, and feedback can be given through forums. Contributors can appeal against the decisions of the Module owner at the Mozilla Foundation. There is no balloting.

4. No geographical limitations apply in development. Firefox is the same everywhere, and it is available everywhere: the Internet is the medium for everything.

5. Because Firefox is OSS, the IPR is open in the development and product/standard phases. In the acceptance phase, proprietary derivates may also be created but Firefox itself is open.

6. Changes follow the process characterized by 1–5. Firefox users can get an automatic update.

7. The source code of the different versions of Firefox is readily available.

8. Firefox is based on open standards, thus enabling an Open Interface.

9. Before a new version is officially released, a test version becomes available. Conformance testing is undertaken by the Firefox community itself. In practice, this turns out to be a feasible approach.

10. The open source nature of Firefox ensures a constant flow of technical support even when there will not be a proprietary derivative. The fact that several small and large companies offer support provides a guarantee that support will be available in future as well.

From the above evaluation we can conclude that the product/ standard phase and the acceptance phase are open but that the development phase is not fully open: in fact, final decision-making is totally closed.

We will now examine whether two common standard war tactics are to some extent present in Browser War II.

Standards war tactics: The pre-emption tactic is not present in the case of Mozilla: the browser is a challenger that has to take on established rivals such as IE. However, we can observe some forms of expectations management. Activities in this respect are not aimed at ensuring that Firefox is winning the browser war against IE: the Mozilla Foundation has been modest in its market share forecasts. It has, however, been fiercely upholding the credibility of Firefox as the best browser, and ensuring that it will continue to be the best browser in terms of security and features. To this end it has ridiculed IE, criticized Opera, and attacked every report that was critical of Firefox's security.

Seven key assets: We will now briefly elaborate on the seven key assets needed to win a browser war, as identified by Shapiro and Varian (1999a).

1. *Control over installed user base*: Firefox is based on open standards and is governed by an OSS license. It is thus non-proprietary and can therefore have no control over the installed user base.

2. *Ownership of Intellectual Property Rights (IPR)*: Firefox is open source: there is no ownership of IPR, in contrast to IE, whose IPR is controlled by Microsoft.

3. *Ability to innovate*: Firefox has been far ahead of IE (Bishop, Seattlepi.com, November 20, 2007).[100]

4. *First-mover advantages*: Firefox had no first mover advantage: IE had an established, dominant position in the market.

5. *Manufacturing capabilities*: Firefox has been developed without much direct cost for the Mozilla Foundation because most contributors were either volunteers or employed by a another partner firm.

6. *Strength in complements*: There are many add-ons available for Firefox, and the number of add-ons is still increasing. The browser does not have a complementary operating system in the way that IE is complementary to Windows, but it is compatible with all operating systems including Windows.

7. *Reputation and brand name*: Although Firefox's reputation and visibility are increasing, Microsoft is better known and has a reputation for getting what it wants. Its products are widely dispersed and it has won a browser war before. On the other hand, the Microsoft image has some negative side effects, and some Microsoft-haters prefer "EBM": "Everything But Microsoft."

Table 7.5 summarizes Firefox's advantageous or disadvantageous position regarding these assets versus IE:

Standardization mechanisms: We will now reflect on whether there are standardization mechanisms present, and how they influence the adoption of Firefox.

1. *Network effects*: Both direct and indirect network effects are present. Given the incompatibilities of the browsers/web pages, these effects benefit the established IE. However, there also seem to be direct network effects at work for Firefox: an increase in the use of the browser makes it more valuable because more web pages will be optimized for the popular browser. This can indeed be noticed: websites are also optimized for Firefox. For example, Microsoft's Live.

Table 7.5 Seven key assets of Shapiro and Varian (1999a): Firefox relative to IE

Seven Key assets	Firefox relative to IE*
Control over installed user base	$--$
Ownership of IPR	$--$
Ability to innovate	$++$
First-mover advantages	$--$
Manufacturing capabilities	$++$
Strength in complements	$+-$
Reputation and brand name	$--$

Note: * $++$, strong advantage; $+$, advantage; $+-$, neutral/no advantage or disadvantage; $-$, disadvantage; $--$, strong disadvantage

com is also optimized for Firefox. Likewise, more add-ons were produced once Firefox became more popular.

2. *Positive feedback*: One would expect that positive feedback, which means that the strong one grows stronger and the weak one grows weaker, would work against the weak challenger Firefox. However, the case of Firefox shows the reverse: "the weak, Firefox, grows stronger."

3. *Lock-in*: The case of Firefox shows that, at this point in time, some users in the browser industry, in particular home users, are willing to adopt another browser, so there is no complete lock-in for IE. IE bookmarks can be easily transferred to Firefox, which removes one possible barrier that could create lock-in. Neither IE nor Firefox require any training in their use. Almost all Firefox users appear to have already used another browser before Firefox and probably still use Firefox in combination with IE. In this sense there is no lock-in for Firefox either. Rather, lock-in to other operating systems than Windows may be a reason to adopt an alternative to IE, and then Firefox becomes the leading browser, maybe not only thanks to its current technical qualities but also because its initial qualities led to positive feedback which increased Firefox market share, which now grows further thanks to network effects in the remaining market segment next to IE's. The positive feedback even leads to a certain shift from IE to Firefox, but without the perspective of a total shift because of the combinations between IE and other Microsoft products.

All individual tables are now integrated into the framework: see Figure 7.2.

Domains	Phases		
	Development	Product / standard	Acceptance
OSS	**OSS origin:** Proprietary based **Development sponsorship:** – *Contribution:* Mostly company sponsored – *Coordination:* Mostly community sponsored	**"Openness" of OSS program** – OSS with proprietary leanings (can be mixed with non-OSS and allows for commercial derivatives **Compatibility of OSS program** – *Between versions:* Compatible – *Between other (non-OSS) products:* IE: mostly compatible **Price of OSS program:** Free **Availability of complements for program:** Many (but no OS) **Quality of OSS program:** High **Availability of support for OSS program:** Reasonable support available.	**Promotion sponsorship:** Both community and company sponsored **Strategic option:** Best Product (Differentiation) and Total Customer Solution	
				Dominant standard *No: about 15% market share*
Standards–setting	**Standards-setting attributes:** **Openness (Krechmer, 2006):** – *Open Meeting:* To some extent – *Consensus:* No – *Due Process:* To some extent – *Open World:* Yes – *Open IPR:* Yes – *Open Change* To some extent – *Effort to standardize:* Joint – *Access to standard:* Open	**Standards-setting attributes:** **Openness (Krechmer, 2006):** – *Open World:* Yes – *Open IPR:* Yes – *Open Change* Yes – *Open Document:* Yes – *Open Interface:* Yes – *Effort to standardize:* Joint – *Access to standard:* Open	**Standards-setting attributes:** – *Mode of standard selection:* Market – *Effort to standardize:* Joint **Openness (Krechmer, 2006):** – *Open World:* Yes – *Open IPR:* Yes – *Open Change* Yes – *Open Document:* Yes – *Open Interface:* Yes – *Ongoing Support:* Yes **Two standards war tactics:** – *Preemption:* No – *Expectations management:* Yes **Seven key assets (Shapiro and Varian, 1999a):** (relative to IE) – *Positives:* Ability to innovate; Manufacturing capabilities – *Negatives:* Control over installed user base; Ownership of IPR; First-mover advantages; Reputation and brand name; Strength in complements **Standardization Mechanisms:** – *Network effects:* Yes (in favor of IE) – *Positive feedback:* Yes – *Lock-in:* Limited (shift to Firefox feasible)	

Figure 7.2 Overview of characteristics of Firefox in Browser War II

8
Standard-Setting Mechanisms in Open Source Software

Winner takes all: key factors affecting Internet Explorer's position in Browser War I

In 1995, Netscape was the dominant standard. According to extant theory, the only possibility for late entrants to win a standards battle is by offering a product with superior quality given its price. However, IE's quality was inferior. Yet IE managed to become the winner in standards war I. Three factors affected IE's position in Browser War I: (1) Microsoft's bundling of IE with Windows; (2) Microsoft's control of key distribution channels through exclusive agreements with ISPs and OEMs; (3) Microsoft's creation and dispersal of proprietary extensions.

The first two factors can be characterized as particularly relating to the standards-setting domain, whereas the last factor particularly relates to the software domain.

(1) *Bundling IE with Windows and* (2) *making agreements with ISPs and OEMs*: To overcome Netscape's huge installed user base, Microsoft targeted new Internet users, the number of whom doubled each year. This next generation of web browser users by and large adopted IE because it was preinstalled "for free" on their PC or came with the CD-ROM from the ISP. The competing Netscape browser had to be downloaded, which was not really difficult but most users simply did not take the effort. By attracting large numbers of new users, IE created network externalities: adoption fostered more adoption as the content of websites was increasingly optimized for IE. The increasing rate of adoption of IE, due to control of the distribution channels, signaled that IE was in a good position to become the dominant

standard and in turn led most web developers to optimize their websites for IE. Bundling IE with Windows and entering into agreements with third parties were arguably the most important reasons that IE became the dominant standard: IE's market share showed a sharp increase after the bundling and agreements with third parties.

(3) *IE created and furthered the dispersion of proprietary extensions*: By adding support for proprietary elements, Microsoft effectively locked in its users. Furthermore, most websites were optimized for IE: webmasters expected IE to become the dominant standard and they could easily design websites for IE by using FrontPage. So they chose IE which Microsoft provided for free, next to IIS. This installed base of complementary products was in favor of IE, despite – at that time – the lower quality of this browser. As a result, web surfers who used IE had no need to change, while Netscape users had a less pleasant browsing experience. In Microsoft's set of software products, the Windows Operating System is the core product. The moneymakers are the Office Suite and the Visual Studio, both connected to Windows. The use of these is stimulated by providing IE and Windows Media Player, but also connected to Windows, for free (Wang et al., 2005).

The three key influencers outlined above helped to seal Netscape's fate by assisting IE to gain significant market share and subsequently creating lock-in and network externalities in favor of IE, which, besides certain other less influential factors, enabled IE to become the dominant standard. Table 8.1 frames the key influencers which explain IE's adoption in the framework.

Table 8.1   Key influencers explaining the adoption of IE

	Phases		
Issues	**Development**	**Product/standard**	**Acceptance**
OSS		(3) Compatibility between other products: Somewhat incompatible.	
Standards-setting		(1) Bundling IE with Windows.	(2) 'Effort to standardize': Exclusive agreements with ISPs, and OEMs. Lock-in and network effects as a result of (1), (2), (3).

Other observations with regard to outcomes

Software – development: The rewritten IE 3.0 enabled higher-paced innovation and better quality, while Netscape's codebase was constraining further innovation, particularly from version 4.0. Furthermore, a huge IE development team, which Netscape could not match, was developing new innovations and proprietary browser standards.

Software – product/standard:

- Price: although believed to be of lesser influence than the key influencers, can still be considered of influence. IE was free. Netscape Navigator copies were only available free to consumers, while Netscape charged corporate end users US$5. Netscape only made its browser available completely free in 1998, when it had already lost a significant amount of market share. Although US$5 per end user is a relatively small amount of money for corporations, it might have been of some influence.
- Quality: By offering a browser that, although initially lower in quality then Netscape, could still be considered a reasonable product, Microsoft prevented the outcome that IE users would become dissatisfied and switch to Netscape. Quality only became better after it was already clear that IE would become the dominant standard. IE 4.0 was the first browser that was considered to be clearly superior to its rival. Although Microsoft did not have a majority of the market share at that time, it was clear that it would be only a matter of time for it to reach an established position. Certainly, in this Browser War I, looking at quality does not help much to explain the outcomes. Quality in the sense of security was also not much of an issue in Browser War I. Microsoft increased investments in browser quality not as part of its battle against Netscape, but once it became clear that a new code engine was needed and the company decided to integrate its browser with its Windows OS. For such integration, a better quality was needed.

Software – acceptance: Microsoft's strategic option for promoting IE is best described by System Lock-in, as this option best explains IE as dominant standard from a strategy point of view. IE's strength in complements (e.g., Windows) and content (e.g., websites) were of vital importance in helping secure its victory.

Standards-setting – all three phases: Microsoft's participation in W3C helped it get its CSS standard accepted. IE had advanced CSS support, which Netscape could not offer. It was from W3C's acceptance of the CSS onwards, and the subsequent release of the CSS supporting IE 4.0, that the Netscape browser versions were considered inferior to the IE versions in terms of features, quality and standard compliance. W3C "has certainly failed to prevent Netscape and Microsoft from developing proprietary versions of HTML. Complaints about the slowness of its procedures are also common. Rather than setting the agenda, critics complain, the W3C is busy trying to keep up with changes driven by the main corporate players. This leads to the charge that, while the W3C appears highly democratic on the surface, its agenda is set by large corporate interests" (Windrum, 1999: 23).

Standards-setting – acceptance: The standard war tactic "Expectations management" can be identified as a relevant factor. Microsoft had built a reputation of becoming market leader in every market it entered, and therefore the announcement that IE aimed to be the preferred browser undermined individuals' and corporations' trust in Netscape as a sustainable dominant standard and thus their willingness to adopt Netscape.

Microsoft did win over a majority of Internet users in a short time by leveraging Windows users over to IE and exploiting its market power over the distribution channels (OEMs, ISPs) to ensure that new users, whose number was doubling per year, would adopt and stick to IE. The adoption of IE was strongly driven by standards-setting-related activities by Microsoft. Network effects and lock-in were spawned on the supplier side by bundling IE with Windows and making agreements with ISPs and OEMs. IE, while generally inferior in quality to Netscape, added proprietary extensions that locked in existing IE users while lowering the compatibility for Netscape users. These standard-setting-related factors enabled IE to become the dominant standard.

Key factors affecting Firefox's position in Browser War II

Four factors have affected Firefox's position in Browser War II: (1) the superior browser-related characteristics, most notably the openness of the license program, its high quality especially with regard to security and features, and standards support, together with a lack of IE innovation; (2) the involvement of commercial companies in both the development and the acceptance phase; (3) the open and collaborative nature of the standards-setting process of Firefox; and (4) the fact that it can be used in combination with operating systems other than Microsoft's.

Factors 1 and 2 can be characterized as particularly relating to the open source software domain. The third factor mainly relates to standards-setting, but this key influencer concerns issues related to the open and collaborative *nature* of the standards-setting process, not so much the standards-setting *activities*. Factor 4 relates to both of these.

1. *Superior browser-related characteristics*: Firefox adopters are attracted by the browser's superior characteristics. The browser scores high on security, offers new features and is standards-compliant. The open nature of the browser allows for customization by the adopter, commercial derivatives and fast bug-fixing. Another advantage is the limited amount of memory needed: the more user "add-ons," the more important this characteristic (IT Productivity Centre, 2007).

In particular, security is an important driver of Firefox's adoption. IE suffered from viruses after security concerns for Firefox in May 2005; the browser's market share even slightly decreased. Microsoft's failure to deliver a high-quality and secure browser can be explained by Microsoft's strategy of tying more and more products to its Windows operating system. This has caused innovation of a large part of the company's software to move at the same pace as the development of the operating system, whose development pace has slowed due to the increasing complexity of the operating system (Lohr and Markoff, 2004).

Another IE-associated factor that might have driven IE users to Firefox is the neglect of pre-SP2 (Service Pack 2) systems. To be best protected against viruses, IE users needed to download and install SP2. This Service Pack, however, required Windows XP. Users with an older Windows version were thus also forced to upgrade to a newer Windows version before being able to install SP2.

2. *Commercial company involvement*: Firefox has been both developed and promoted in an open and collaborative nature by the Mozilla

Foundation, volunteers, and commercial firms. In particular, the involvement of commercial firms, next to the OSS community, is considered key to Firefox's success.

In the development phase, commercial firms were involved in the development of Firefox by offering engineers, money and/or code. This ensured the continuity of the project, and enhanced the quality of the browser. Without contributions from these firms, it is unlikely that the browser would ever have become an alternative to IE.

In the acceptance phase, companies were in different ways involved in the promotion of Firefox. This involvement opened up possibilities of promoting which would not have been possible for the Mozilla Foundation as such. Moreover, it generated extra credibility and visibility for the product. By providing commercial derivates for which support is offered and which are part of a broader package, firms like IBM and Red Hat advanced the adoption of Firefox among corporations. Google has sought to increase Firefox diffusion among consumers by including the browser in Google Pack, rewarding every Firefox download that includes its toolbar, and having further optimized some of its services for Firefox. These companies are not altruistically inspired in their support, but act to exploit a win–win situation where a good quality and high diffusion of Firefox are also in their best interest. More specifically, these companies might be motivated to strengthen Firefox to avoid vendor-dependence and standards lock-in, to exploit opportunities for commercial marketing of the browser, to have a good browser to complement their software package, or to have a browser running on their Linux system (IBM, Red Hat). In the end, the involvement of commercial companies can thus be traced back to the fact that Firefox is OSS.

From a corporate users' point of view, choosing Firefox is an approach of not being dependent on one major supplier, Microsoft, but instead using a product that is supported by several companies, thus ensuring less dependency. Apart from this rational argument, feelings of discomfort with Microsoft might play a role for some users.

3. *The open and collaborative nature of the standards-setting process*: The collaborative and mostly open approach of standards-setting of Firefox relates strongly to issues addressed under key influencers 1 and 2. It identifies issues from the standards-setting viewpoint which explain the favorable browser-related characteristics in terms of quality and features. The openness of the standard further explains the involvement

of firms, and in turn the positive effects with regard to quality and promotion that follow from that involvement.

Because there is a significant overlap with issues identified and addressed under the respective phases for the Standards-Setting and OSS domain, this factor will not be addressed in depth.

4. *Compatibility with other than Microsoft's operating systems*: Because IE was not available for Apple and Linux users, these had to choose another browser. Firefox was one of the candidates. In terms of the theory, the installed base of users of a complementary product favored the product compatible with their own. Firefox's multi-platform compatibility widens not only the potential pool of adopters but also the developer community willing to contribute towards the development of Firefox. The involvement of firms like Red Hat and IBM may be explained by the fact that Firefox can also run on Linux.

Table 8.2 Key influencers explaining the adoption of Firefox

	Phases		
Issues	**Development**	**Product/standard**	**Acceptance**
OSS	(2) Development sponsorship: – *Contribution: mostly company sponsored*	(1) Superior product-related characteristics compared to IE: openness (license), quality, security, compatibility/ standards-support (4) Compatibility also with other operating systems than Windows	(2) *Promotion sponsorship*: Involvement of commercial firms
Standards-setting	(3) *Effort to standardize*: Joint (with firms) (3) *Access to standard*: Open	(2) included in Google Pack and commercial packages (as derivate) (3) *Access to standard*: Open	(3) *Effort to standardize*: Joint (with firms)

Other observations with regard to outcomes

OSS development

OSS origin: the predominantly proprietary origin of Firefox has several qualities that in this case help explain the success of the browser. The browser's commercial legacy (the Gecko codebase) proved to be important because it indirectly ensured the high quality of Firefox for the following reasons:

1. The Gecko codebase was modular and thus allowed for the contribution of dispersed individual volunteers and company developers. What was true for Linux applied to Firefox: "Without modularity, there was little hope that contributors could understand enough of the design to contribute in a meaningful manner, or develop new features and fix existing defects without affecting many other parts of the design. Linux *needed* to be modular to attract and facilitate a developer community" (MacCormack et al., 2004: 27).

2. The new codebase offered new opportunities for innovation, as it was not constrained any more by old code.

3. Major parts of code now underlying Firefox had been developed by Netscape earlier on, which ensured that it was complete. Anecdotal evidence suggests that the major reason for open source project failure is a lack of contributors to do the work (West, 2003a). Vital, but very time-consuming and monotonous, development is often not carried out, thus leading to an incomplete and/or flawed product. Another problem that often plagues OSS projects that are developing a program from scratch is "branching," the evolution of incompatible versions during development. The commercial legacy of Gecko provided the Mozilla project with a complete and trustworthy basis to build on.

These effects cannot directly be contributed to the proprietary origin, but to the fact that the browser's code – when it was still proprietary – was rewritten from scratch mostly by Netscape developers.

Development sponsorship: The reason why the Firefox browser did not share the fate of many other OSS projects that never took off is also thought to lie in the involvement of firms in the development contribution, as noted above. On top of the observations made in this section, we will offer some additional remarks below.

Companies could become involved in the development of Firefox due to the project's open nature. By participating, they could contribute to the development of a high-quality product as an alternative to IE that was also compatible with their products.

The absence of significant entry barriers – aside from engineering expertise – led to the participation of many and different types of contributors to an OSS project: hobbyists and professionals, organizations and individuals (Egyedi and van Wendel de Joode, 2004). Incompatibility lurks due to the different levels of competence and motivation of contributors and the less controlled approach of development. Moreover, open-source development may fragment the design into competing versions (Kogut and Metiu, 2001: 257). Firefox's "by invitation only" meritocracy avoided this pitfall: only the valuable contributions of a small group of key developers were accepted. This approach safeguarded the quality and continuity of the project. The community-driven coordination further prevented any one company from having an excessive say in the direction of the project, as was the case in the pre-Mozilla.org phase when Netscape was the only sponsor. In line with this, one might speculate that success of the project might also be explained by the fact that there was no "over-involvement" of one or more companies in the development, as was the case with the Netscape/AOL involvement in the Mozilla project, prior to its spin-off. As outlined in the Halloween Memos, Netscape reserved the final right to reject or force modifications into the Mozilla codebase (Valloppillil, 1998). The Halloween Memos further note that "Linus Torvald's management of the Linux codebase is arguably directed towards the goal of creating the best Linux. Netscape, by contrast, expressly reserves the right to make code management decisions on the basis of Netscape's commercial/business interests. Instead of creating an important product, the developer's code is being subjugated to Netscape's stock price" (Raymond, 1998b; Valloppillil, 1998). Mockus et al. (2002: 343) further note that "in commercial development, feature content is driven by market demands, and for many applications such as browsers, the market generates great pressure for feature richness." This pitfall can indeed be observed during the pre-Mozilla.org phase of the project, during which the Netscape-sponsored Mozilla Suite suffered from high code complexity due to feature richness, which eventually led to the development of Firefox.

Besides the likelihood of a low quality product, one can further speculate that over-involvement, meaning one company as main and only sponsor, will lower the amount of contributions of both volunteers and commercial firms to the project. The Mozilla project only became successful after its independence, which suggests that Netscape's overinvolvement was counterproductive and hindered the development of a successful browser.

In the development of Firefox, most substantial contributions were company-sponsored and coordination mostly community-sponsored. This balanced combination ensured that the commercial interests of one company could not be decisive. In the case of Firefox, corporations are also driven by their own interests in contributing. These interests are, however, reconciled with the interest of the browser, as the final coordination is carried out by the independent Mozilla Foundation platform. The Mozilla Foundation has the ultimate say and can thus overrule commercially inspired contributions of company contributors that might harm the browser.

OSS product/standard

Openness (license): The MPL license which governs Firefox allowed for commercial derivates and mixing with proprietary software. These characteristics invited contributions from firms and other developers. In the previous Netscape phase, these had been hesitant because the NPL gave Netscape the right to distribute/relicense code contributed by others to third parties on a commercial basis. The company involvement also explains the "closed/proprietary" leaning of the OSS program. It could also have opted for GPL, but commercial derivatives and combining OSS with non-OSS would have been impossible.

Compatibility: With regards to compatibility with other browsers, the incomplete compatibility with IE hinders adoption of Firefox. On a different level, with regards to compatibility with the OS, IE is only compatible with a Windows-based operating system, while Firefox is compatible with Windows, Linux and Apple's operating system. Firefox is the default browser of Red Hat and Suse Linux.

Quality: The high quality with regard to security and the innovative features of Firefox can be related to both the fact that the browser is OSS and the fact that it is based on a new codebase. Firefox's design is less susceptible to viruses compared with IE. The new codebase also allowed for the inclusion of new features such as tabs. Firefox's better security and features due to its design can thus not be attributed solely to the fact that it is OSS: this could also hold for a non-OSS program with a new design that offered the same or a better level of innovation and security. However, the open nature of the browser can also help explain the better security and more innovative features of Firefox. Firefox's security is enhanced by the availability of the source code, which enables a more rapid detection of flaws. The extended OSS development community enables a fast supply of patches. The collective and open development of Firefox further utilizes the collective creative power of the Firefox developer community, which will most likely give it a significant supply of contributions, of which it can pick the best. As explained above, the high quality can to some extent also be explained by company involvement.

The characteristics of "price," "availability of support" and "availability of complements" relative to IE are not thought to be critical in explaining the success of Firefox. "Availability of support" is assured for a longer period because of the free availability of the software and the involvement of various small and big companies. Should some of these cease their support of Firefox, others will continue. In the case of IE, there is a dependency on Microsoft. However, we found no evidence that this argument in favor of Firefox plays an important role.

OSS acceptance

The promotion sponsorship by both firms and the OSS community helped the adoption of Firefox. The Mozilla Foundation has become a visible platform that has promoted Firefox to consumers on the basis of "differentiation."

The reasons for commercial firms to promote Firefox are primarily because of the browser's Product/Standard-related characteristics. These allowed companies to combine Firefox with its proprietary software, and thus helped to complement and optimize its other product offerings to corporate customers. The browser further allowed the creation of commercial derivatives and prevented vendor dependence.

Standards-setting: all three phases

It is interesting to note that Firefox also engaged in collaborative standards-setting activity with its competitor Opera in WHATWG to develop new open standards.

The network effects in the browser industry mostly work to Firefox's disadvantage and to IE's advantage, although Firefox now has gained some threshold that might also create network effects in favor of the browser. There is no positive feedback for IE, which benefits Firefox, as well as the fact that there seems to be no complete lock-in for IE. In the market segment of users with another operating system than Windows, Firefox is the dominant standard and here it profits from network effects and positive feedback. The adoption of Firefox so far can primarily be explained by characteristics related to the browser, especially its open nature, high security, standards support, and compatibility with different operating systems. These characteristics can at least be explained partially by the fact that Firefox is an OSS program. The open nature of the browser ensured open standards support and enabled collaborative standards-setting by the OSS community as well as firms. Company involvement in the development as well as promotion proved to be particularly important to the "success" and the adoption of Firefox.

The influence of OSS on standards-setting

Development phase

When comparing the "evaluation of characteristics" for the standards-setting behavior and characteristics of IE and Firefox in the development phase, several differences can be observed. IE's development was closed and carried out only by Microsoft. In the case of Firefox, the development of the standard is open and collaborative in terms of the framework, access to the standard, and joint effort to standardize. These characteristics are inherent to OSS, so this is not surprising. What is less typical is that the development is not completely open according to Krechmer's openness requirements, and it is not only carried out by the OSS community, but commercial firms such as IBM play a major role. The initiators of the Firefox project decided to limit the openness of the development process because a "meritocracy" would safeguard the quality of the project. The openness in the development of Firefox contributed to its quality and security, also because user feedback could be incorporated at short notice. The limitations to the openness assured coherence, avoided a proliferation of versions, and protected the product against obstruction and amateurism.

Product/standard phase

In the Development Product/Standard phase, both IE and Firefox were involved in activities to develop standards defining the compatibility of the browser in a standards-setting body or workgroup. In these actions incompatibility was at stake – the incompatibility both of their own browser and of the rival's browser. Microsoft's participation in W3C ensured the acceptance of its CSS standard, which subsequently made Netscape's browser more incompatible. After the standard was accepted, Microsoft later on added proprietary extensions that caused further incompatibility. Firefox – being OSS – strived after compatibility by adhering to open standards. To advocate and further develop open standards, it joined efforts with Opera and Apple in WHATWG. There thus seems to be a shift from striving for browser incompatibility (proprietary extensions, IE in Browser War I) to striving for browser compatibility (open standards, Firefox in Browser war II).

Another difference between IE and Firefox is that, as IE is governed by a proprietary license, the access to its standard source code is closed, whereas Firefox's OSS license stipulates that access to the standard is open.

Acceptance phase

In the acceptance phase, the standards-setting for IE and Firefox can be characterized for both as market-oriented, but in different ways. The extent and type of collaboration were distinctively different. In the case of Firefox, there was no explicit contract-related collaboration as was the case with IE's agreements with ISPs and OEMs. Also, the collaborators were different for Firefox, whose corporate supporters were mostly search engines and Internet content companies, or vendors of suites such as IBM, attracted for different reasons by the open nature of the browser. Firefox was promoted by the small Mozilla organization, by the (broad) community, and, last but not least, by the commercial firms that remained loyal to the product.

In the case of Firefox there was, furthermore, no presence of standards-war tactics to the extent Microsoft engaged in during the Browser war I. Remarkably, there is in general no decisive presence of favorable standardization mechanisms for Firefox, because network externalities in favor of IE seem to be mitigated by a lock-in caused by the installed base of a complementary product: the operating system. Moreover, switching costs are not so high that switching is hardly possible. The latter fact is partly due to standard characteristics related to OSS. This can be regarded as a strong deviation from Browser War I, in which the above mechanisms greatly aid any explanation of IE's success.

When one compares the key influencers of IE in Browser War I with Firefox in Browser war II, one can note a shift in the nature of key influencers from being standards-setting-related to OSS: the rise of IE can be explained by standardization mechanisms related to the standards-setting activities of Microsoft, not by the quality of the browser. Firefox's adoption, however, cannot be explained by favorable standardization mechanisms espoused through standards-setting activities by the program's promoters, but can largely be explained by superior product-related characteristics, which in turn, to some extent, can be explained by the fact that Firefox is OSS.

On an even more general level, one can note what seems to be a shift in adoption from "supplier push" for IE in Browser War I to "demand pull" for Firefox in Browser War II. As outlined above, in Browser War I the standards-setting activities of Microsoft, creating network effects, drove adoption of IE. In Browser War II, the adoption of Firefox seems primarily driven by its better product-related characteristics, and not so much by the standards-setting activities of the Mozilla Foundation or corporate sponsors. One can speculate that here adoption can thus be explained by "demand/user pull."

Conclusions

Standards-setting for IE can be by and large typified as closed, non-collaborative, and involving many standards-setting activities by

Microsoft. The influence of OSS led to a collaborative and an open, but in some important aspects not open, standards-setting process, with company involvement and fewer standards-setting activities for Firefox. When comparing the key influencers of the two cases, we claim that there has been a shift from a "supplier push" approach in Browser War I to a "user pull" approach in Browser War II.

9
What can be Learnt from these Browser Wars

Impact of OSS on competitive dynamics and outcomes in the market

At this juncture we ask: *How does OSS change standards-setting activities?* We argue that OSS changes the approach of standards-setting in the first place because of its open, but not necessarily completely open, collaborative development and joint promotion of an open standard, in contrast to mostly solitary development and single-company promotion of a closed standard in cases of proprietary software. The open license allows for access to the source code, and the modification thereof, thus allowing an open and collaborative approach of development and subsequent promotion. The license in the case under study allows for commercial derivatives and the combination with proprietary software. The open standard can then also serve as the basis for a proprietary, competing standard, such as Netscape's Mozilla derivative in the second browser war. The license thus makes it attractive for firms to participate in the standard's development and promotion.

A second impact of OSS on the approach of standards-setting is related to possible company involvement, next to involvement of the open source community, in development and promotion of the standard. In the Firefox case we found extensive company involvement in development as well as promotion. Such involvement is atypical of most OSS projects studied in academic literature so far. The findings of this study suggest that company involvement can be key to the standard's success. This is in line with Dedrick and West

(2004), who note that, when support for the OSS project from a major corporation like IBM or HP is evident, it is more likely that OSS will be adopted by a corporation. The findings of this study further suggest that, when certain restrictions are placed on the contribution to the development of the standard, although it is open, the standard is more likely to succeed than would be the case in a purely open manner of development of the standard. The above observations on this "open but not completely open" manner of development and the role of core developers are in line with research carried out by Krishnamurthy (2002). Based on a study of the top 100 mature products on Sourceforge[1], Krishnamurthy found that the vast majority of mature OSS programs are developed by a small number of individuals. Many OSS projects have a small group of core developers who do most of the research and decide which code is included, although other developers play important roles by contributing fixes and testing (Scacchi et al., 2006).

A third element of the influence of OSS on standards-setting is related to the OSS-standards-setting context with multiple "standard-setters" with multiple motives for sponsoring the development and promotion of the standard. Not all development sponsors are also promotion sponsors but, at least in our case, all major promotion sponsors are also development sponsors. The standards-setters do not collaborate in a "formal consortium," but in a more loosely organized manner. These standard-setters have multiple motives for developing and/or promoting an open standard, ranging from offering a product (Mozilla Foundation), to creating commercial derivative (e.g., Netscape), to combining it with their software packages (e.g., IBM), to avoiding standard lock-in (e.g., Google). Some of the sponsors in the development phase thus become competitors later on.

A fourth element of the impact of OSS concerns the standard's adoption. In the case of OSS, switching costs can be minimal. Therefore, the lock-in mechanism is less important. For the same reason, network effects and positive feedback are less decisive. Then other features attract more emphasis. In the Firefox case, this concerned the superior quality of the standard and this quality was further enhanced by the OSS character. Therefore, this study suggests a return to "classical theory" to explain the ability of a late OSS entrant to gain some foothold through superior quality of the standard rather than through standardization mechanisms.

We further ask: *How does OSS shape competitive dynamics and outcomes in the market?* We believe, based on the evidence presented above, that OSS changes competitive dynamics by serving as a competitive tool with multiple applications for firms. The open standard weakens vendor dependence, avoids standards lock-in, and provides a cheap product that can swamp competitors who charge money for their product and that can be used for the firm's product offerings so there is no need to license a proprietary alternative anymore. Firms can thus use OSS to strengthen their competitive position *vis à vis* rivals who only compete with proprietary standards, and with proprietary software vendors. OSS might further be valuable for companies that compete on Total Customer Solution as identified by Hax and Wilde (1999).

A firm's involvement in OSS may be interpreted as a form of co-opetition as defined by Nalebuff and Brandenburger (1997). By collaborating in the development of the program it creates a "bigger pie" with regard to the company's products or services and saves on the cost of development. The company subsequently has to ensure that it indeed captures a significant part of this pie. The release of some of the source code by a firm may also be regarded as co-opetition. By releasing the source code the company hopes to create greater value down the road by creating opportunities for the firm's products or services. A firm may further collaborate if the OSS program can be regarded as a "complementor" to the firm's product offerings; including the product of the complementor makes customers value the firm's product even more.

Open access to a technology or standard leads to a shift from competition to become the dominant standard (i.e., inter-standard competition) to competition over the open standard (i.e., intra-standard competition) (Besen and Farrel, 1994). So, besides competition between an open and a proprietary standard for the establishment of a technology as the dominant standard, there will also be competition between firms within the open standard; its specifications should fit the specific requirements of the firm, for example, to combine the OSS with a complementary product offered by that firm.

OSS changes outcomes; *ex ante* literature on the diffusion of technological innovations under conditions of increasing returns to adoption, and lock-in (Arthur, 1989 and David, 1985), predicts that in the long term a single dominant technology will prevail, which, once established, prevents competing technologies from obtaining a foothold in the market (Bonaccorsi et al., 2004). However, the findings of this study suggest that a late entrant OSS program can to some extent overcome the network externalities enjoyed by a dominant standard, by its open and product-related characteristics, and obtain a foothold in the market. However, this does not imply that OSS will be able to displace a proprietary dominant standard with a large, locked-in installed user base, if its adoption is only driven by these product-related characteristics and the product does not come preinstalled. The proprietary rival can further discourage the adoption of its OSS rival by increasing its product quality to a level almost comparable to that of the OSS program. The findings of this study suggest that the open nature of a high-quality OSS product will ensure a certain degree of coexistence. This seems to be in line with research carried out by Casadesus-Masanell and Ghemawat (2006) on the competitive dynamics of software wars between Microsoft Windows and Linux, where "in the absence of cost asymmetries and as long as Windows has a first-mover advantage, *Linux never displaces Windows of its leadership position*, [...] regardless of the intrinsically better design and potential differential value of Linux." In the case of an operating system, switching costs for migrating to a competing standard are high. In our case, the barriers to switching are lower. For several customers it may be risky to depend on software from one dominant supplier: they may prefer to spread risk and, additionally or exclusively, use OSS.

The literature has further recognized that firms that adopt an open standard policy are more likely to succeed in obtaining an installed user base, because an open standard is more likely to attract producers of complementary products and customers who want to avoid dependence on one firm (Farrell and Gallini, 1988; Farrell and Saloner, 1986; Hayashi, 1992).

OSS does not aim for proprietary lock-in but supports open standards. As it does not lock in its installed user base, one can speculate that a dominant OSS product may therefore be more easily forced out of the market by a proprietary rival product of superior quality and with network effects in its favor. Our case confirms the findings of Bitzer and Schroder (2004) that if, through the entry of OSS, the software industry segment moves from a monopoly to a duopoly, the level of innovation increases because the proprietary firm's position cannot be taken for granted any longer.

We therefore conclude that, based on the two cases presented above, OSS changes the manner of standards-setting and the role of standardization mechanisms, standard quality and standard openness in the standard's adoption. The openness of the standard as well as the standards-setting processes with regard to OSS is a key driver of this change in standards-setting. The openness of the standard allows for, besides other factors, the involvement of companies. This, in turn, stimulates quality in the development as well as adoption through promotion of the standard by third parties.

Based on the cases discussed above, this study suggests that the adoption of an open standard and the decrease in market share of proprietary standard cannot be adequately explained by standardization mechanisms only. It appears that certain product characteristics of the OSS program, some of them unique to OSS, help in the case under study to explain the adoption of an open standard in what was regarded as a locked-in, winner-takes-all market with an established dominant proprietary standard. OSS is further found to be both a threat as well as an opportunity to software firms in the industry. It can be a threat to firms whose business is based on the possession and exploitation of a proprietary standard, while involvement in OSS offers new opportunities for firms with regard to product offering and services.

Although OSS is "here to stay" and has significant market potential, it is unlikely that a late OSS entrant will be able to displace a proprietary dominant standard with a substantial installed user base, merely through favorable product-related characteristics. This study foresees that the introduction of OSS in the software industry will lead to a coexistence with, but not a displacement of, the dominant proprietary software.

Some concluding remarks

A platform battle again

The Browser War I was much more than a competitive battle for web browser market share: it was essentially a battle for dominance in the operating system market as well, where Netscape and Sun were aiming to turn the browser into an operating system versus Microsoft's efforts to prevent the integration of the browser and the operating system to maintain the leverage of its operating system and prevent the rise of a browser-based platform that would pose a threat to its operating system. The browser war between IE and Firefox is again much more than a battle for market share; it is also a battle for the browser platform upon which most of the Web 2.0 applications will run. Web 2.0 refers to web services that allow people to collaborate and share information online. With Web 2.0, a browser receives (through, for example, the interactive AJAX technology that is based on open standards, supported by many browsers and platforms) a functionality comparable to the functionality of an operating system. Consequently, it can function as a platform for web-based applications, that is, a web-based platform that runs in the browser and is written in the language of the browser, rather than of the operating system (Managing Technology @ Wharton, 2005).[2] This creation of a new "web-based ecosystem" (Greene, 2005), where the browser, not the Windows operating system, will be the application's platform, clearly undermines Microsoft's business model. It seems thus warranted to conclude that more is at stake than just the browser market shares. It is interesting to note that for Web 2.0 a browser that supports open standards seems vital, because proprietary standards supported by a browser such as IE can stifle innovation. There is also the possibility that Microsoft, through adding proprietary extensions to now open Web 2.0 standards, can limit the functionality of services of rivals such as Google. As Windrum notes, "ensuring the set of underpinning standards remains open property is the best means of guaranteeing freedom of competition between the applications built on the core standards" (Windrum, 1999: 24). Open standards further allow for customization, which is key for Web 2.0, which is all about customizing and personalizing web content for each user. It also allows other developers to build upon these types of services (e.g., on Gmail). Most Web 2.0 stakeholders (e.g., Ebay, IBM, Google with Google Maps and Gmail) have themselves therefore aligned with Firefox, which supports open standards and has excellent AJAX support. They do not want to become dependent on IE. So this development can be part of the explanation for the active support of these companies and can be an important argument in favor of Firefox in the near future.

Rewrite necessary

Firefox's codebase (Gecko) was completely rewritten, which is one of the reasons for its high quality. Proprietary software programs that have already been on the market for a significant time, like IE, can often be constrained by their code, as the code becomes more complex over time and does not allow for the inclusion of new technologies or functionalities that were not foreseen when the original program was written. An OSS program with a new codebase is not hindered by these code restraints and can offer more features and/or better quality than its proprietary counterparts. Indeed, in the case of IE, fundamental design decisions for IE prevented the addition of tabs and other features as in Firefox without a thorough update of Windows (Chakraborty, 2004).

Microsoft now seems to find itself in the same position as Netscape in late 1995, when Microsoft made a risky but strategically wise decision to redesign the IE code from the bottom up. Cusumano and Yoffie (1998) note that this decision meant delaying the release of IE 3.0, but the resulting product was technically far superior (in potential) to Netscape's Navigator, and the IE code was long overdue for a redesign in which security (not really an issue when IE 3.0 was designed) would be integral (Chakraborty, 2004). Firefox was the challenger with new, clean code that enables a higher level of security. The fact that Microsoft will start to supply preinstalled free anti-virus and anti-spy software with Vista suggests that the company indeed cannot improve the security of IE and is therefore forced to treat symptoms rather then cure the disease. Either way, Microsoft has announced that it will make security a top priority in developing the new Internet Explorer 8.0 browser.[3]

It therefore seems warranted to conclude that an existing proprietary software program, or more specifically the code-engine of a browser, should be "redesigned", also termed "re-architectured", from scratch from time to time in order to enable fast-paced innovation, to ensure high quality and to keep up with OSS rivals. Otherwise, the browser software will sooner or later run into its limitations.

Google

Google is a formidable player in the Internet industry, as well as a stakeholder in the second browser war. On top of the observations already made, it is interesting to note that the Google Toolbar might also be used to download software. Enabled by the broadband Internet that allows for large downloads, a web browser can then also be used as a way to distribute software (e.g., Google Pack or Firefox). This might be a way to displace software that comes preloaded on the PC. Google may also develop its own browser, based on Firefox, to integrate all its other services. Google Desktop can be seen as a first step in this direction (IT Productivity Center, 2007).

The outlook for Firefox

One can speculate on the prospects for Firefox in Browser War II. Firefox's fate is intertwined with the success of IE 8.0. The success of IE 8.0 in turn will depend on the extent to which the browser improves compatibility, security and quality (Desmond, 2008).[4] IE 8.0 is said to improve quality and security, but time will tell if this is enough. As IE 8.0 will also be released as a stand-alone browser, users with an older Windows version are thus not forced to upgrade to a newer Windows anymore. This might also boost IE's market share.

A large group of browser users do not really seem to care too much about quality, security or features. It therefore seems unlikely that Firefox will be able to overcome the network effects of IE's installed user base only by being a better and open standards-supporting product. To increase its adoption and create network effects, Firefox should come preinstalled on PCs. The browser's market share might further be increased when more commercial firms adopt Firefox as their default browser. The latter appears unlikely because many companies are dependent on IE for their internal web-based (network) applications. An adoption of Firefox would force them to redesign those systems. Users, both corporate and non-corporate, could, however, use Firefox alongside IE for their web browsing.

The way in which Internet standards evolve will be vital. If they become more open due to Firefox's pressure and/or Web 2.0 requirements, and more websites are also optimized for open standards, the adoption of Firefox as well as other OSS browsers based on open standards might increase.

Firefox is not likely to be forced out of the market. The browser is supported by some key Microsoft rivals and is expected to continue offering a high level of quality and security that make a minority of Internet users value the browser over IE. This study therefore deems it likely that Firefox will coexist with the dominant standard IE in the web browser industry, achieving a niche position with a market share of about 10% to 30%. It is, however, doubtful that Firefox, under the current conditions, will displace IE as the dominant standard, but its current market share in some European countries, such as Finland and Slovenia, shows that this is not impossible. A full replacement is not feasible; many users do not have clear preferences as long as a technology works, so they will not make a shift towards Firefox. Another, small, group of users apply both browsers in one PC.

Theoretical implications

This study aimed to examine unexplored perspectives in the literature by combining literature and insights relating to OSS with the literature on standardization and applying these to the case of web browser wars. The preceding and following sections highlight some implications for academic theory and provide direction for future research.

The findings in this study on OSS and standards-setting point to the role of firms, the open – but not completely open – development, and the role of standardization mechanisms. These issues need to be further examined through future research. The findings further show how the openness of standards of a late entrant OSS program can – to a certain extent – overcome the network externalities of a proprietary incumbent who produces the dominant standard. Additional research is needed to systematically test our findings in other cases. A distinction may be made between OSS and proprietary software on different levels – for instance, server (Apache – Windows Server), operating system (Linux – Windows), browser (including for instance, Safari and Opera) – and what might be potential explanations for similarities or differences. Future research on Firefox might further cover the presence and functioning of collaborative innovation and technological succession in the context of complex technology as formulated by Windrum (1999).

Practical implications

When faced with an OSS rival, a firm should consider the position of its proprietary program in terms of product-related characteristics (e.g., quality, security, price/costs), but particularly in terms of network effects-related issues (installed user base as percentage of the market, growth of market, lock-in, switching barriers) and the disruptive potential of its OSS challenger in this respect. A company should further assess what holds more value: supporting an open standard/OSS and thus foregoing the possibility to appropriate, but creating new sources of revenue via services or commercial derivates; or continuing to exploit a proprietary standard and reap the benefits thereof. If a company wants its dominant standard to stay closed, it should ensure a reasonable level of quality and security of its program, and exploit network effects to prevent the adoption of a current or potential OSS rival. Companies could further participate in an OSS project to support related products as complements or services.

Firms offering proprietary applications software thus have three basic options with regard to access to their standard/source code: (1) release their source code; (2) release parts of their source code (for example Microsoft Shared Source); or (3) grant no access whatsoever to the source code.

Companies could further use OSS as a means of strategic renewal, as IBM did, and use OSS as a competitive tool.

Non-software firms should consider adopting OSS or stressing the need for open standards-based software because it is ultimately in their interest to support open standards rather than proprietary technology, mainly to avoid business dependence on one single software supplier, in many cases Microsoft.

With regards to the second browser war, Microsoft ought to strengthen IE's position by (1) offering a reasonable level of quality by mimicking Firefox's features and a significantly higher level of security to prevent defection of current users; (2) innovating, developing new standards; (3) ensuring that IE continues to come as the preinstalled, default browser on PCs; (4) preventing adoption of Firefox by companies and government institutions, who account for many users; (5) seeking to discredit Firefox by highlighting its weaknesses, especially when security is concerned, and touting new IE versions; and (6) preparing for the mobile market.

The Mozilla Foundation and Firefox supporting firms should (1) seek to get Firefox pre-installed on PCs more often, for example as part of Google Pack. In this regard, OEMs could thus use Firefox as a bargaining chip, to put pressure on Microsoft; (2) strike deals with large corporations and government institutions; and (3) ensure that Firefox continues to be the "best and safest browser."

Companies should seek to reduce their dependency on one browser and company, and make their new software packages Firefox compatible as well.

Limitations of this study

There are certain limitations of this study that should be taken into account. These limitations can be grouped into three categories: the Theoretical framework, the Case, and the Approach.

Theoretical framework: The framework is broad in scope, incorporating multiple concepts and theories, to substantiate the explorative nature of the study. The drawback of this broadness is the complexity of the analysis that comes with it. The overlap between the two domains also makes it harder to examine how they interrelate.

Despite this broadness, the framework provides only one lens to look at the reality and might therefore have excluded possibly relevant factors. "Environmental" factors such as technology infrastructure, for example, are not included in the framework; the rise of Firefox might also have been facilitated by, for example, higher download speeds, as was the case in the first browser war, and more experienced browser users, fewer Internet novices than was the case in first browser war.

Moreover, the framework seems to have limited potential to capture and analyze dynamism in a systematic and consistent manner; by means of the evaluation of characteristics, the framework mostly captures moments in time, meaning not differences in quality, but just quality at one point. Although it takes into account the subsequent versions of the same program/standard, it is not well suited to capturing these dynamics. This limitation can, however, be addressed; in the "Evaluation of characteristics," changes in issues (e.g., quality) between two versions can be indicated by arrows.

Future studies should further develop adequate measures to quantify and measure the involvement of firms in an OSS project.

Case and data: The first caveat is that Browser War II is still unfolding. Observations and analysis thus pertain to a situation that has not completely crystallized yet, although it provides enough important clues for meaningful analysis. Furthermore, the main focus of the second case is on the two most important browsers: the established proprietary incumbent, and the late entrant OSS challenger. Although attention is paid to other proprietary browsers, their influence is not thoroughly analyzed. Google Desktop, for instance, might turn out to become a serious competitor of Firefox. One should further note that its proprietary origin and company involvement make Firefox an atypical OSS project. The data on the web browser market share/installed user base does not allow for making a distinction between old and new browser users, or between corporate users and consumers. This deficiency limits a full analysis of the extent to which these account for Firefox's adoption, and what the influence of OSS is on this. Finally, field research among users might have revealed motives for browser adoption.

Approach and focus: This study has adopted a fairly broad theoretical scope, covering many issues. This is inherent in the exploratory nature and goal of this research. Due to the study's qualitative nature and the number of parameters covered, unambiguous cause–effect relations are hard to expose. Follow-up research should therefore be more focused, possibly concentrating on a few factors or a single phase. Future research should further test whether findings hold for a different case. Hypotheses and propositions can be derived from the study and subsequently tested. It might also be insightful to frame the first browser war and/or the second or other standards wars in a quantitative model. Models might, for example, test the effects of installed user base-related advantages and network effects versus open standards and higher quality and security in standards-setting. Summarizing, we can conclude that the findings of this study shed more light on the case under examination and enrich the *ex ante* literature with new (theoretical) insights. They should, however, not be regarded as definitive, and should serve as a starting point for further more specific and more in-depth research. The framework should further be applied to other cases, to see whether the findings differ, and to identify the drivers of these differences.

Appendix
Worldwide Market Share

Different sources provide different figures about web browser market shares, depending on both the method of measuring and the sample chosen. Given the amount of data on which the statistics are based, Xiti[1] seems to be the best source. Table A1 provides data for the period September 2006–September 2007. However, earlier data were not available. Xiti provides data per country and per continent. The indicator per continent is an average of the indicators of the countries in that continent. Due to this method, data of small countries contribute too much and data of large countries too little to the overall result. The same applies to Xiti's World indicator: it is the average of the continents. Oceania, which may be expected to have a small number of PC users and a relatively low market share for IE, thus causes the final figure for IE to be too low. The September 2007 data are based on visits to 110,337 websites (See Table A1).

OneStat.com[2] provides data for a longer period. Market shares for June 2007 is provided in Table A2.

A share of x% for browser Y means that x% percent of visiting Internet users arrived at sites that are using one of OneStat.com's services by using browser Y. All numbers mentioned in the research are averages of the last week of June 2007, and all measurements have been normalized to the GMT timezone. Research is based on a sample of 2,000,000 visitors divided into 20,000 visitors of 100 countries each day. The same source provides the following additional data as shown in Table A3.

Cheng (2006)[3] shows the data as in Table A4.

Janco Associates' IT Productivity Center (2007; 2008)[4] provides rather different data:

The reason for the deviation from the above figures might be that Janco Associates captures its data from a limited number of sites which are primarily used by professional business users, not consumers. However, the tendency is the same; diminishing market

Table A1 Web browser market shares in percentages of visits, World Index

	2006				2007								
	September	October	November	December	January	February	March	April	May	June	July	August	September
IE	81.07	80.78	80.21	80.04	80.06	80.27	79.03	78.14	77.34	76.53	76.23	75.97	74.65
Mozilla	14.86	15.16	15.85	16.01	16.03	16.03	17.20	18.09	18.82	19.60	19.93	20.18	21.33
Safari	1.68	1.71	1.72	1.73	1.76	1.68	1.77	1.79	1.86	1.83	1.83	1.84	1.96
Opera	1.42	1.39	1.33	1.29	1.28	1.26	1.31	1.36	1.37	1.37	1.38	1.38	1.42
Netscape	0.68	0.69	0.68	0.75	0.70	0.61	0.57	0.49	0.48	0.54	0.50	0.49	0.50
Camino	<0.1	<0.1	<0.1	<0.1	<0.1	<0.1	<0.1	<0.1	<0.1	<0.1	<0.1	<0.1	<0.1
Sony PSP	<0.1	<0.1	<0.1	<0.1	<0.1	<0.1	<0.1	<0.1	<0.1	<0.1	<0.1	<0.1	<0.1
AvantGo	-	-	-	-	-	-	<0.1	<0.1	<0.1	<0.1	<0.1	<0.1	<0.1
Other	0.25	0.22	0.16	0.14	0.13	0.11	0.07	0.08	0.07	0.07	0.04	0.06	0.07

Source: Xiti, 2007.

Table A2 Web browser market shares in percentages, June 2007

Browser	Worldwide	USA	Canada	Australia	UK	Germany	France
IE	84.66	75.69	75.76	66.42	86.00	68.84	83.32
Firefox	12.72	19.65	16.47	26.32	11.22	26.69	14.05
Safari	1.79	3.77	5.72	1.86	1.61	1.25	1.68
Opera	0.61	0.61	0.69	4.05	0.53	1.88	0.78
Netscape	0.11	0.17	0.13	0.24	0.10	0.19	0.09

Source: OneStat.com.

Table A3 Web browser market shares in percentages, 2002–2007

Browser	2002[a]	2003[b]	2004[c]	2005[d]	2006[e]	2007
IE	96.6	95.4	93.6	85.5	85.2	84.7
Mozilla / Firefox	–	1.6	2.1	11.5	12.2	12.7
Safari	–	–	0.7	1.8	1.6	1.8
Netscape	2.1	2.5	–	0.3	0.1	0.1
Opera	0.4	0.6	1.0	0.8	0.7	0.6

Source:
[a] http://www.onestat.com/html/aboutus_pressbox4.html, last visited December 15, 2007.
[b] http://www.onestat.com/html/aboutus_pressbox23.html, last visited December 15, 2007.
[c] http://www.onestat.com/html/aboutus_pressbox44-mozilla-firefox-has-slightly-increased.html, last visited December 15, 2007.
[d] http://www.onestat.com/html/aboutus_pressbox40_browser_market_firefox_growing.html, last visited December 15, 2007.
e http://www.onestat.com/html/aboutus_pressbox49-microsoft-internet-explorer-7-usage.html, last visited December 15, 2007.

Table A4 Web browser market shares in percentages, September 2005–September 2006

Browser	9/05	12/05	3/06	6/06	9/06
IE	86.87	85.05	84.70	84.04	82.10
Firefox	7.55	9.57	10.05	10.77	12.46
Safari	2.39	3.07	3.19	3.19	3.53
Netscape	2.16	1.24	1.05	0.93	0.85
Opera	0.51	0.55	0.54	0.57	0.64
Mozilla	0.42	0.41	0.34	0.31	0.25
Other	0.08	0.11	0.12	0.19	0.15

Source: Cheng, 2006.

Table A5   Web browser market shares in percentages, September 2006–March 2008

Browser	9/06	9/07	3/08
IE	73.43	63.86	60.00
Firefox	11.75	17.40	19.95
Safari	1.12	1.05	1.65
Netscape	10.21	10.71	9.68
Opera	0.78	1.87	1.17
Mozilla	0.99	1.40	1.32
Google Desktop	1.74	2.38	4.01

Source: Janco Associates' IT Productivity Center (2007; 2008).

Notes

1 Introduction

1. Onestat.com Press Box (Onestat.com) (2002) April 29, 2002, from www.onestat.com/html/aboutus_pressbox4.html, last accessed July 17, 2008.
2. Xiti Browsers Barometer (Xitigroup.com) (2007) from www.xitimonitor.com/en-us/browsers-barometer/index-1-2-3-0.html, last accessed July 17, 2008.

2 Open Source Software

1. Software can be transmitted in either "source code" or "object (or binary) code." Programmers write software in the form of a source code using programming languages such as Basic and Java. To run as a program, the source code then needs to be decoded into binary code, the sequence of 0s and 1s that directly communicates with the computer. The binary code is difficult to interpret and modify, in contrast to the source code which allows for direct modifications (Lerner and Tirole, 2004). The binary code can be regarded as the back of an embroidery: it is hard to make sense of. One needs (to see) the front of the embroidery to interpret and modify the program. Commercial software vendors usually supply customers only with the binary code.
2. The open source movement was not the first movement that proposed free access to source codes. Credit for the first push to "free the code" goes to the Free Software Foundation (FSF) established in 1985 by Richard Stallman, a programmer at MIT's Artificial Intelligence Laboratory. Stallman was particularly worried by the trend in the software industry at that time towards development of proprietary software. The FSF was founded to develop and diffuse a legal mechanism that could preserve free access for all to software developed by other (individual) programmers. The idea of free software was never really accepted: the industry was suspicious of it (von Hippel and von Krogh, 2004) and Stallman's anti-capitalist rhetoric didn't help either to increase adoption among users and developers.
3. Those project leaders are often the ones who created an initial, basic version of the program, and who provide the general vision about the direction and properties of the program (Mendys-Kamphorst, 2002).
4. Shared Source is an open source-like form of code sharing which is generally more restrictive than true open source, but less so than proprietary code. See www.opensource.org/docs/sharedsource.php, last accessed on July 17, 2008. For a critical review of Shared Source from an open source movement's point of view.

5. See www.microsoft.com/resources/sharedsource/Licensing/default.mspx for an overview of the license programs, last accessed on January 10, 2008.

6. Microsoft released also some of its code for an internally developed product under an open source license. Until then Microsoft had made its source code only available under a variety of "shared source" licensing mechanisms (Foley, 2004).

7. The large number of different open source licenses reflects the different opinions on these two issues. A complete overview of the licenses can be found on the website of the Open Source Initiative (www.opensource. org/licenses, last accessed on July 17, 2008). The website counts more than 50 licenses. Most licenses are an elaboration of one of the two most popular OS licenses: the General Public License (GPL) and the Berkeley Software Distribution (BSD) license (Egyedi and van Wendel de Joode, 2004). It is beyond the scope of this study to provide an extensive overview of the legal nature of OSS; see for more on the legal aspects of open source licensing Lerner and Tirole (2002), Frost (2005), and Kennedy (2001).

8. In case of *commercial software*, other software licenses apply. The software is typically only available as binaries to end users. By the way, according to the FSF (www.fsf.org, last accessed on July 17, 2008), "commercial" and "proprietary" are not the same: "Most commercial software is proprietary, but there is commercial free software, and there is non-commercial, non-free software."

   Trial software offers limited usage of software package in terms of time and/or features. It is intended to persuade users to purchase the full software package.

   Freeware is software made available free of charge. It may be used for free. It is distributed in binary form only.

   Royalty-free libraries is software whose binary and source code may be freely used and distributed but whose source code may not be changed by the user.

9. The MPL referred to here concerns version 1.1 developed by the Mozilla Foundation. The license can be found at www.mozilla.org/MPL/MPL-1.1.html.

10. The Netscape Public License (NPL) was developed by Netscape and contains special prerogatives that apply only to Netscape. The license allows Netscape to re-license code covered by the NPL to third parties under different terms. This condition was necessary to satisfy the proprietary contracts between Netscape and partner companies. The license also granted Netscape the right to use code covered by the NPL in other (proprietary) Netscape products, without those products falling under the NPL. This would essentially mean that contributions of outside programmers to the source code could be "internalized" and "commercialized" by Netscape. Opposition from the OSS community led Netscape to develop the MPL, which does not grant Netscape the right to use code contributed by outsiders. Developers can, however, still license their contributions to the Mozilla source code under the NPL license.

11. Making changes to open source products and then not contributing those changes back to the developer community, but rather attempting to keep them proprietary for commercial purposes or other reasons (Hecker, 2000).
12. According to a July 2005 article on Computerweekly.com, Microsoft has hired software engineers from the OSS world to improve compatibility between its Windows systems software and open source technology (particularly Linux) (Computerweekly.com July 26, 2005).
13. By selling OSS on CD-ROM. This software can still be downloaded for free from the Internet.
14. For instance, www.sourceforge.net, last accessed December 8, 2007.
15. The other three contributions are: (1) align these strategic options with a firm's activities; (2) introduce adaptive processes to help company respond to an uncertain environment; and (3) align aggregate and granular metrics to strategy (Hax and Wilde, 2001).

3 Standards and Standards-Setting

1. Van der Kaa combined the definitions of Garud and Kumaraswamy (1993) and De Vries (1998). Antonelli (1994: 197) defined compatibility standards as standards that "enhance or make possible (technical) coordination among different components of a (technological) system" (brackets added by the authors).
2. Farrell and Saloner (1988: 236) define the bandwagon mechanism as follows: "If an important agent makes a unilateral public commitment to one standard, others then know that if they follow that lead, they will be compatible at least with the first mover, and plausibly also with later movers."
3. Oshi and Weeber (2006) consequently apply the standards-setting attributes to the case of the standardization battle for the WID-OS to examine the cooperative and competitive actions of the main players.
4. See Stango (2004) for a thorough discussion of the literature on standardization mechanisms and the economics of standard wars.
5. One should note that, although there is resemblance between the two, network effects should not be equated with "economies of scale". Economies of scale result from (production) size rather than – as is in the case of network effects – interoperability. A more precise approach to refer to the economies of scale as they are commonly conceived and "network effects" is by distinguishing between "demand side" and "supply side economies of scale" (Katz and Shapiro, 1986). "Classical" economies of scale, where benefits are garnered due to size efficiencies, take place on the supply/production side, while network effects arise on the demand side and are a function of the numbers of users of a good or service. Although not completely the same, the terms "network effects" and the more narrow "network externalities" are used interchangeably. See Egyedi and Van Wendel de Joode (2004) for a detailed overview of

standardization in OSS development theory on (positive) *network effects*.

6. Klemperer (1987) as quoted in West (2003a: 319) classifies switching costs into three categories: First, "transaction costs (e.g., the cost of uninstalling equipment from one supplier and installing equipment from a new supplier); second learning costs (e.g., PC usage skills); and finally contractual costs, or costs deliberately introduced by suppliers (e.g., frequent flyer programs)." In the case of software especially numbers two and one (in that order) are barriers to switching to another software product.

7. According to Windrum (2004), in his study on the browser war between IE and Netscape, conventional theory identified four ways in which a new technology entrant can overcome the network externalities enjoyed by firms producing a dominant market standard. "First, the new technology variant is superior to the old technology. Second, the new technological variant is more price competitive. Third, the firm that develops the new technology enjoys a distribution advantage over the firm(s) producing the dominant technology. Fourth, the firm exploits advertising to gain competitive advantage" (Windrum, 2004: 387).

4   Standardization Battles in OSS: A Theoretical Framework

1. Collaboration in the development phase can also be viewed as collaboration between OSS programmers working on the same product to prevent "forking" (the evolving of one "root version" into a different incompatible and competing version). This study will, however, limit collaboration to collaboration between the OSS community and commercial companies.

5   Industry Background

1. "Still later, after its DOS operating system was succeeded by the backward-compatible Windows, it became the Wintel (Windows/Intel) standard" (Bresnahan and Greenstein, 1999: 14).

2. IBM attempted to regain market share by introducing the PS/2 computer as a proprietary standard. The attempt failed, as the new standard did not offer quality advantages (Ehrhardt, 2004).

3. Gaudin, S., November 29, 2007, HP grabs punishing lead over Dell in PC market share, www.computerworld.com/action/article.do?command= viewArticleBasicandtaxonomyName=laptopsandarticleId=9049999andt axonomyId=76andintsrc=kc_top, last accessed December 8, 2007.

4. The latest numbers from the US Census Bureau report more than 40,000 firms in the industry as from 2000 (www.census.gov, last accessed November 24, 2007). The latest version (dated 2007) of the Software 500

(published by www.softwaremag.com) provides an overview of the biggest and most successful firms (in different parts) of the industry.

5. An "operating system" is a software program that controls the allocation and use of computer resources (such as central processing unit time, main memory space, disk space, and input/output channels). The purpose is to support "the functions of software programs, called 'applications', that perform specific user-oriented tasks", like displaying text on the screen. The operating system supports the functions of applications by exposing interfaces, called "application programming interfaces", or "APIs." (Penfield Jackson, 1999: 2)

6. Searchwindevelopment.com, http://searchwindevelopment.techtarget.com/sDefinition/0,,sid8_gci211708,00.html, last accessed on November 16, 2007.

7. Interestingly, in May 1999, Microsoft lawyers and Princeton professor Edward Felton spent hours arguing about the definition of "Web browser" in preparation for Microsoft's antitrust trial. Microsoft said that because Internet Explorer is so firmly integrated into the operating system, it is not a single application program and thus blurs the lines, while Felton argued that Internet Explorer is an application program like any other (Thurrot, 1999).

8. In preparing this section we used "A brief history from the browser wars" by Corts and Freier (2003), www.quirksmode.org/browsers.

9. Not to be confused with the World Wide Web (WWW, also nicknamed Internet) that also was created by Berners-Lee.

10. Cailliau, R., A little history on the world wide web, www.w3.org/History.htm, last accessed December 8, 2007; Berners-Lee, T. and Fischetti, M., *Weaving the Web The original design and ultimate destiny of the World Wide Web,* Collins: New York, 2000.

    Gromov, G.R., History of Internet and WWW: The Roads and Crossroads of Internet History 1995–1998, http://netvalley.com/intvalold.html, last accessed December 8, 2007.

11. The National Center for Supercomputing Applications (NCSA), based at the University of Illinois at Urbana-Champaign, aims, according to its website (www.ncsa.uiuc.edu), to be a leader in the development and deployment of new computing and software technologies for the scientific and engineering community. Special emphasis is placed on the development of a (national) cyber-infrastructure for science and engineering.

12. Ives, B. and Jarvenpaa, S., Virtualschool.edu, 1994, What is the Internet and the world wide web?, http://virtualschool.edu/mon/CaseStudies/WebCase/www.html, last accessed December 8, 2007.

13. http://biztech.ericsink.com/Browser_Wars.html, last accessed December 8, 2007 (for a firsthand account of Browser War from the viewpoint of an Spyglass insider).

14. www.websidestory.com, last accessed December 8, 2007.

15. http://64.233.169.104/search?q=cache:Qdu1PNViy7IJ:www.websidestory.com/company/news-events/press-releases/view-release.html%3Fid%3D1063%26year%3D2002+the+percentage+of+daily+internet+users+

worldwide+that+access+the+internet+trough+a+particular+browseandh
l=nlandct=clnkandcd=1, last accessed December 8, 2007.

16. Xiti provided data from 151,729 websites generated visits between October 1, 2006 and October 31, 2007.

17. www.cnn.com/TECH/computing/9810/08/browser.idg/, last accessed December 8, 2007.

18. http://news.netcraft.com/, last accessed December 8, 2007.

19. Xiti Browsers Barometer (Xitigroup.com) (2007). Retrieved December 8, 2007 from www.xitimonitor.com/en-us/browsers-barometer/index-1-2-3-0.html.

20. In this XiTi Monitor study, the indicator of a continent is meant to be representative of the countries audited from it. This indicator is an average of the indicators of the countries. Thus, the behavior of a country that generates few visits intervenes fairly in the behavior of its continent.

21. www.onestat.com, last accessed on December 2, 2007. In the methodology used, a global usage share of x percent for browser Y means that x percent of the visitors of Internet users arrived at sites that are using one of OneStat.com's services by using browser Y. All numbers mentioned in the research are averages of the last week of June and all measurements are normalized to the GMT time zone. Research is based on a sample of 2,000,000 visitors divided into 20,000 visitors of 100 countries each day.

22. www.onestat.com/html/aboutus_pressbox53-firefox-mozilla-browser-market-share.html, last accessed on December 2, 2007.

23. Keizer, G., Linuxworld, Fix Firefox's memory problems, says Mozilla director, November 14, 2007, www.linuxworld.com.au/index.php/id;2067098313;fp;4;fpid;4, last accessed December 5, 2007.

24. Infoworld.com, May 31, 2006. www.infoworld.com/article/06/ 05/31/ 78797_HNballmerrandd_1.html?BUSINESS%20CHANGE%20 MANAGEMENT, last accessed November 26, 2007.

25. Google Annual Report 2006, www.propeller.com/viewstory/2007/03/02/ here-it-is-googles-annual-report-2006/?url=http%3A%2F%2Fwww.sec.g ov%2FArchives%2Fedgar%2Fdata%2F1288776%2F00011931250704449 4%2Fd10k.htmandframe=true, last accessed November 26, 2007.

26. Microsoft Annual Report 2007, www.microsoft.com/msft, last accessed November 26, 2007.

27. "In a distributed computing system, middleware is defined as the software layer that lies between the operating system and the applications on each side of the system." (http://middleware.objectweb.org, last accessed on 26 November, 2007). Middleware, by making APIs available, offers independent software vendors (ISVs) the chance to write applications that can work with many operating systems.

28. API stands for Application Programming Interface. An API is "An interface for letting a program communicate with another program. In web terms" (Eggheaddesign.co.uk, www.eggheaddesign.co.uk/glossary.aspx, last accessed on November 16, 2007). In other words, it is the interface that a computer system, library or application provides in order to allow

requests for services to be made of it by other computer programs, and/ or to allow data to be exchanged between them. One of the secondary purposes of an API is to describe how computer applications and software developers may access a set of (usually third party) functions (for example, within a library) without requiring access to the source code of the functions or library, or requiring a detailed understanding of the functions' internal workings.

29. In US law having a monopolistic position (70% of market share) is not illegal; however, using this position to restrain free trade in another market is (Cushman and Sanderson King, 2003).

30. See Gilbert and Katz (2001) for an analysis and interpretation of the economic issues raised in *the U.S.A. v. Microsoft* case.

31. For a timeline of the *U.S. v. Microsoft* antitrust case, see www.wired.com/ news/antitrust/0,1551,35212,00.html, April 11, 2002.

32. BBC News, September 17, 2007. Microsoft loses anti-trust appeal, http://news. bbc.co.uk/2/hi/business/6998272.stm, last accessed November 26, 2007.

33. Lawsky, D. October 22, 2007, Microsoft finally bows to EU antitrust measures. http://investing.reuters.co.uk/news/articleinvesting. aspx?type= tnBusinessNewsandstoryID=2007-10-22T114840Z_01_ BRE001179_RTRIDST_0_BUSINESS-MICROSOFT-EU-DC.XML, last accessed November 26, 2007.

34. BBC.com (2005) "The assault on software giant Microsoft," May 9, 2005, http://news.bbc.co.uk/1/hi/business/4508897.stm, last accessed on November 14, 2007.

35. BBC.com (2005) "How Microsoft plans to beat its rivals," May 10, 2005, http:// news.bbc.co.uk/1/hi/business/4516269.stm, last accessed November 14, 2007.

36. http://opensource.feratech.com/halloween/halloween1.php, 2005, last accessed November 26. 2007. The document contained references to a second memorandum specifically dealing with Linux, and that document was also obtained, annotated and published by Raymond as Halloween II.

37. FUD stands for "Fear, Uncertainty, and Doubt." FUD was first defined by Gene Amdahl after he left IBM to found his own company, Amdahl Corp.: "FUD is the fear, uncertainty, and doubt that IBM sales people instill in the minds of potential customers who might be considering Amdahl products." (www.catb.org/~esr/jargon/html/F/FUD.html, last accessed December 16, 2005). It is a term popular within the open software community, used to describe tactics to scare people away from adopting OSS products, by sowing Fear, Uncertainty and Doubt about OSS products.

38. During the *U.S.A v. Microsoft* antitrust trial, Intel Vice President Steven McGeady testified that "Microsoft hopes to 'embrace, extend and extinguish' competition by substituting the company's proprietary software for the public-domain, open technologies that have driven the frenetic growth of the Internet." (ZDNET News, November 8, 1998).

39. http://news.bbc.co.uk/1/hi/business/4516269.stm, BBC.com, "How Microsoft plans to beat its rivals," May 10, 2005, last accessed December 8, 2007.

40. www.microsoft.com/windowsserversystem/facts/default.mspx, last accessed November 26, 2007.

41. www.microsoft.com/resources/sharedsource/Initiative/FAQ.mspx, July 23, 2007, last accessed July 17, 2008.

42. www.microsoft.com/resources/sharedsource/Articles/Microsoft andOpenSource.mspx, last accessed July 17, 2008.

43. www.mozilla.org/free-faq.html, last accessed December 8, 2007.

44. A rendering engine, or layout engine, is a software engine that converts HTML code into visual web pages. Trident is the rendering engine for IE, Presto for Safari, and Webcore for Opera.

45. XML user interface language that allows single development of a user interface that runs on Windows, Macintosh and Linux.

46. Note that Mozilla itself is thus not a web browser; it is an open source web development project (further) developing source code for the Mozilla Application Suite programs (www.mozilla.org, last accessed December 8, 2007). A program is generally described as "Mozilla-based" when it is based on software code whose development is facilitated through the Mozilla Foundation. Mozilla can refer to the Netscape Mascot, Mozilla Suite, the Mozilla project, or Mozilla-based browsers. Mozilla also refers to the original code as released by Netscape. This study, when mentioning Mozilla, refers to the Mozilla Foundation or Mozilla Corp., unless indicated otherwise.

47. www.mozilla.org/reorganization/, last accessed December 8, 2007.

48. www.mozilla.org/products/choosing-products.html, last accessed December 8, 2007. (The Mozilla Suite is not a combination of Firefox and Thunderbird: according to the Mozilla.org website it is "a completely different application".)

49. The Mozilla Foundation continues to maintain Mozilla 1.7, the latest version of its Suite, as it is still being used by many corporate users (www.mozilla.org/seamonkey-transition.html, last accessed December 8, 2007).

50. www.mozilla.org/projects/seamonkey/, last accessed December 8, 2007.

51. www.mozilla.org/press/mozilla-2005-02-16.html, last accessed December 8, 2007 and www.mozilla.org/press/mozilla-2005-10-19.html, last accessed December 8, 2007.

52. www.betanews.com/article/Mozillas_Firefox_usage_estimates_climb_by_15_M_since_July/1196713676, last accessed December 8, 2007.

53. These download counts did not include downloads using software updates and downloads from third-party websites.

54. Cabello, P. Mozillalinks, November 24, 2007. Next steps for Firefox, http://mozillalinks.org/wp/2007/11/next-steps-for-firefox-3/, last accessed December 8, 2007.

6   Browser War I (1995–1999): Microsoft Versus Netscape

1. An extensive description of how Microsoft initially did not recognize the potential of the Internet can be found in Business Week's "Inside Microsoft" article of July 15, 1996.
2. www.quirksmode.org/browsers, last accessed November 25, 2007.
3. www.blooberry.com/indexdot/history/ie.htm, last accessed November 25, 2007.
4. www.holgermetzger.de/Netscape_History.html, last accessed November 25, 2007.
5. CSS = Cascading Styling Sheets: a language that lets designers separate the visual definition of a web page from its content. See the next page for more explanation .
6. VBScript = Visual Basic Scripting Edition: an *interpreted script* language from Microsoft that is a subset of its *Visual Basic* programming language designed for interpretation by Web browsers.
7. By contrast, Jenkins et al. (2004) state that IE 3.0 and Netscape 3.0 can be considered to be almost equal in quality.
8. www.quirksmode.org/browsers, last accessed November 25, 2007.
9. www.blooberry.com/indexdot/history/ie.htm, last accessed November 25, 2007.
10. www.quirksmode.org/browsers, last accessed November 25, 2007.
11. Document Object Model (DOM) is a "browser-neutral application programming interface (API) that lets web authors use scripts to automatically update parts of a Web page with fresh information" (CNET News, April 7, 2004). Various interfaces were initially implemented by web browsers to manipulate elements in an HTML document through JavaScript. This prompted the World Wide Web Consortium (W3C) to come up with a series of standard specifications that defined the W3C Document Object Model (W3C DOM). These specifications are platform and language-independent and "provide a standard set of objects for representing HTML and XML documents, a standard model of how these objects can be combined, and a standard interface for accessing and manipulating them" (www.w3.org/TR/REC-DOM-Level-1, last accessed July 17, 2008).
12. www.quirksmode.org/browsers, last accessed July 17, 2008.
13. www.quirksmode.org/browsers, last accessed July 17, 2008.
14. CNET News, (2003), "W3C releases scripting standard, caveat", January 9, 2003, http://news.com.com/2100-1023-979976.html, last accessed November 15, 2007.
15. W3Schools.com, www.w3schools.com/browsers/browsers_stats.asp, last accessed November 16, 2007.
16. Cornell University, http://iws.cit.cornell.edu/iws2/technology/techinfo.cfm, last accessed November 16, 2007.

17. www.w3.org/Style/CSS/Disclosures, last accessed November 16, 2007.
18. www.holgermetzger.de/Netscape_History.html, last accessed July 17, 2008.
19. Hecker, F. June 20, 2000. Setting Up Shop: The Business of Open-Source Software, www.hecker.org/writings/setting-up-shop, last accessed January 8, 2008.
20. www.catb.org/%7Eesr/writings/cathedral-bazaar/cathedral-bazaar/ar01s13.html, last accessed July 17, 2008.
21. For an elaborate description of (events prior to) the source code release, see Hamerly et al. (1999).
22. www.catb.org/%7Eesr/writings/cathedral-bazaar/cathedral-bazaar/ar01s13.html, last accessed July 17, 2008.
23. There are no network effects with regard to training: both IE and Netscape require little training to use.

7   Browser War II (2003–2008): Mozilla Versus Microsoft

1. www.blooberry.com/indexdot/history/ie.htm, last accessed on November 16, 2007.
2. "A layout engine takes content (such as HTML, XML, image files, applets, and so on) and formatting information (such as Cascading Style Sheets, hard-code HTML tags, etc.) and displays the formatted content on the screen. The layout thus provides the foundation needed to display content on the screen, including a complementary set of browser components. However, Gecko does not package all of these components alongside other interface modules in a coherent, user-friendly Web browser application (including menus, tool bars, etc.), such as Mozilla or Netscape Navigator." (www.mozilla.org/newlayout/faq.html, last accessed July 17, 2008). This is done by Mozilla.org which assembles the necessary components into Mozilla Firefox.
3. www.mozilla.org/newlayout and www.mozilla.org/roadmap/roadmap-26-Oct-1998.html, last accessed July 17, 2008.
4. www.mozilla.org/newlayout/faq.html, last accessed July 17, 2008.
5. www.catb.org/%7Eesr/writings/cathedral-bazaar/cathedral-bazaar/ar01s13.html, last accessed on July 17, 2008.
6. The project was first called Phoenix. Later (from version 0.6) the name was (due to legal issues) changed to Firebird, and has then evolved into Firefox since version 0.8 in 2004.
7. The Mozilla Firefox Development Charter explicitly states that the project aims to ensure that the download size stays under 5.0MB on Windows for the installer (www.mozilla.org/projects/firefox/charter.html, last accessed July 17, 2008). By committing to this small size the program is kept downloadable and nimble.
8. KHTML = KDE's HTML: is the HTML layout engine developed by the KDE project. It is the engine used by the Konqueror web browser, and a forked version (WebKit) is used by Apple's Safari web browser.

9. *CNET News*, December 8, 2005 and *CNET News*, July 26, 2005.
10. *CNET News*, April 2, 2003. Mozilla.org had already stated in a development roadmap that the next version of its browser would be based on Phoenix.
11. www.mozilla.org/projects/firefox/roadmap.html, last accessed December 8, 2007 and www.mozillazine.org/, last accessed December 8, 2007. Please check the latest minutes of the regular Mozilla.org staff meetings for the most recent developments.
12. Cabello, P. Mozillalinks, November 24, 2007. Next steps for Firefox, http://mozillalinks.org/wp/2007/11/next-steps-for-firefox-3/, last accessed on December 8, 2007.
13. For more on Mozilla's development, technology and architecture: see Shaver, M. and Ang, M., May 29, 2000, Inside the Lizard A Look at the Mozilla Technology and Architecture, www.mozilla.org/docs/ora-oss2000/arch-overview/moz-arch-overview.pdf, last accessed on January 8, 2008. For more specifics on Mozilla's development model: "Free/Open Source Software Development" edited by Stefan Koch; Mockus et al., (2002)
14. http://www.mozilla.org/mission.html, last accessed at November 26, 2007.
15. See www.mozilla.org/owners.html, last accessed July 17, 2008. For an overview of the owners and Eich, B. and Baker, M. Mozilla "super-review," www.mozilla.org/hacking/reviewers.html, last accessed January 8, 2008 for a list of the super code reviewers.
16. If differences arise between a contributor and a module owner, mozilla.org makes the "final call" (Hamerly et al., 1999). The foundation has "the ultimate decision-making authority, retains the right to designate and remove module owners" and has also the right to determine the direction of the project, the code included in the code repository, and the process by which the project is run (Mockus et al., 2002; Baker, 2004).
17. Anyone is allowed to make their own distribution and include code that did not make it into the official Mozilla.org release.
18. www.mozilla.org/hacking/code-review-faq.html, last accessed July 17, 2008.
19. www.mozillazine.org/talkback.html?article=6203, last accessed July 17, 2008.
20. Ross: Mozilla was a technology platform aimed at software vendors who would customize, repackage and market it to a number of different audiences. It made sense to build a platform as feature-rich as possible so that vendors could pick and choose the features they wanted with ease. It made less sense to focus on perfecting the user interface, because "perfection" was decided by the population who would ultimately use it, and this population varied among the software vendors who leveraged the platform. Phoenix, the then name for what is now called Firefox (authors' comment), on the other hand, sought to cut out the middle man and market directly to an audience. Since this audience was primarily

non-technical in character, we felt it necessary to judge patches not just on technical merit but also on how closely they adhered to this new vision. Code+UI review, however, took more time than we were willing to spend in our eagerness to develop Phoenix quickly. So we sought to find the people who understood our vision so well that they didn't need this additional layer of review, and then bring them onto the team. (Ross, 2005)

21. www.mozillazine.org/talkback.html?article=6203, last accessed July 17, 2008.

22. www.mozilla.org/mission.html, last accessed November 26, 2007.

23. Krishnamurthy (2005a: 29): "closed door projects are defined as those that provide access to the program and source code to any interested person, but do not provide access to core functions of software development (esp. setting up roadmaps, checking code and submitting patches)." Krishnamurthy further provides five explanations as to why groups may organize in this way.

24. The old code was too tightly coupled for would-be contributors to modify without having to examine its potential impact on many other parts of the system.

25. On May 8, 2005 the Mozilla Foundation instituted a Mozilla Community Awards program to recognize the dedicated community of contributors.

26. www.slate.com/id/2103152/, last accessed July 17, 2008.

27. www.mozillazine.org/talkback.html?article=6203, last accessed July 17, 2008.

28. See http://mozilla.org/credits/, last accessed January 8, 2008 for Mozilla contributors.

29. www.mozilla.org/about/fast-facts, last accessed July 17, 2008.

30. http://loosewire.typepad.com/blog/2005/02/interview_with_.html, last accessed November 26, 2007.

31. http://steelgryphon.com/blog/index.php?p=37, last accessed at November 26, 2007.

32. http://steelgryphon.com/blog/index.php?p=34, last accessed November 26, 2007.

33 http://steelgryphon.com/blog/index.php?p=34, last accessed November 26, 2007.

34. http://steelgryphon.com/blog/?p=39, last accessed November 26, 2007.

35. Including a bug that could allow attackers to secretly run malicious software on PCs (*CNET News*, September 21, 2005).

36. http://secunia.com/product/11/, last accessed July 17, 2008.

37. http://secunia.com/product/4227/, last accessed July 17, 2008.

38. McHugh, J., 2005, "The Firefox explosion," Wired Magazine, issue 13.02, www.wired.com/wired/archive/13.02/firefox.html?pg=2andtopic=firefo xandtopic_set, last accessed November 14, 2007.

39. Wagner, J., 2005, IBM Donates code to Firefox www.internetnews.com/ xSP/article.php/3527341, August 15, 2005, last accessed November 16, 2007.

40. www.mozilla.com/en-US/firefox/2.0.0.9/releasenotes/, last accessed November 26, 2007.
41. www.mozilla.org/support/firefox/faq#free, last accessed July 17, 2008.
42. www.mozilla.org/reorganization/, last accessed July 17, 2008.
43. According to www.mozilla.org/MPL/FAQ.html#7, from January 31, 2005, "the GNU Library General Public License was also developed by the Free Software Foundation. It is similar to the GPL, but it introduces the idea that a library of functions covered by the LGPL may be used by a program without the program being a derivative work of the library. This allows the program to be issued under different terms than the LGPL. This makes the LGPL less restrictive (the developer is compelled to release the source code to less of his work) than the GPL," last accessed November 26, 2007.
44. The license can be found on www.mozilla.org/MPL/MPL-1.1.html, last accessed November 15, 2007. Further information on the licenses can be found on www.mozilla.org/MPL and www.mozilla.org/MPL/license-policy.html, last accessed November 26, 2007.
45. http://moz.sillydog.org/archives/netscape_9_will_support_firefo.php, last accessed on November 26, 2007.
46. The NPL further stipulated that changes to files contained in the source code were considered modifications and were covered by the NPL. New files that did not contain any of the original code or subsequent modified code are not considered modifications and are not covered by the NPL (Hamerly et al., 1999).
47. www.mozilla.org/MPL/relicensing-faq.html, last accessed November 15, 2007.
48. www.mozilla.org/MPL/relicensing-faq.html, last accessed November 15, 2007.
49. www.mozillazine.org/talkback.html?article=4155, last accessed November 15, 2007.
50. Mozilla.org, www.mozilla.org/MPL/NPL-1.1.html, last accessed November 16, 2007.
51. www.mozilla.org/foundation/trademarks/policy.html, last accessed November 15, 2007.
52. Firefox add-ons can be found on: https://addons.mozilla.org/?application=firefox, last accessed January 8, 2008.
53. www.crn.com/sections/breakingnews/dailyarchives.jhtml?articleId=168600040, last accessed November 16, 2007.
54. www.mozillazine.org/talkback.html?article=6900, last accessed July 17, 2008.
55. Netscape Navigator up to version 4.7 was also responsible for massive proprietary extension of the core web standards, but was not criticized for this as much as IE.
56. Microsoft, http://msdn2.microsoft.com/en-us/library/ms970422.aspx, last accessed November 16, 2007.

57. www.techworld.com/applications/news/index.cfm?NewsID=5604, March 21, 2006, last accessed November 26, 2007.

58. XUL (XML User Interface Language) is a user interface description language used for creating user interfaces with Mozilla's Cross Platform Front End (Mozilla.org, July 25, 2007) to support Mozilla applications like Mozilla Firefox and Mozilla Thunderbird. While XUL is not a public standard, it reuses many existing standards and technologies, including CSS and JavaScript.

59. WHATWG = Web Hypertext Application Technology Working Group: in contrast to the vendor-neutral W3C, the WHATWG working group is vendor-driven, with three organizations that provide browsers as main contributors: Mozilla Foundation, Opera Software, and Apple Computer. The working group does not mean to override the W3C: the standards proposals created by the WHATWG are submitted to the W3C for approval or amendment. The working group also intends to work more closely with the W3C in future.

60. www.mozilla.org/about/fast-facts, last accessed July 17, 2008.

61. A list of sites non-compliant with W3C (but with IE proprietary standards), which are thus not viewed correctly in Firefox, can be found on http://www.defendingthefox.com, last accessed January 8, 2008. Websites that can only be viewed with IE include the popular Expedia, and, less surprisingly, the Windows Update site.

62. http://developer.mozilla.org/en/docs/Firefox_1.5_Beta_for_Developers, last accessed November 16, 2007.

63. MSDN IEblog (2006), http://blogs.msdn.com/ie/archive/2006/08/22/712830. aspx, last accessed November 16, 2007.

64. www.nu.nl/news/1354239/52/Opnieuw_mededingingsklacht_tegen_Microsoft.html, last accessed December 13, 2007.

65. www.blooberry.com/indexdot/history/ie.htm, last accessed November 26, 2007.

66. or more on the community-led marketing campaign accompanying the launch of Firefox, see Krishnamurthy (2005a/b).

67. As counted by a link search on Google: www.google.com/search?hl=enandq=link%3Awww.mozilla.org%2Fproducts%2Ffirefox%2FandbtnG=Search and www.google.com/search?q=link%3Awww.mozilla. organdbtnG=Google+Search.

68. www.mozilla.org/about/staff, last accessed July 17, 2008.

69. www.mozilla.org/about/timeline, last accessed November 15, 2007.

70. www.mozilla.org/press/mozilla-2005-08-03.html, last accessed November 26, 2007.

71. www.mozilla.org/reorganization/, last accessed November 15, 2007.

72. Meyer D., ZDNet Asia.com, www.zdnetasia.com/news/software/0,39044164,62032062,00.htm, last accessed November 26, 2007.

73. *CNET News*, November 26, 2005 and www.mozilla.com/press/mozilla-2005-12-2.html, last accessed November 15, 2007.

74. www.theinquirer.net/?article=28380, last accessed July 17, 2008.

75. www.theregister.co.uk/2007/05/02/dell_ubuntu_analysis/, last accessed January 12, 2008.
76. Foley, M.J., ZDNet, May 1, 2007. What's next up for Internet Explorer? Microsoft opens up (a little) http://blogs.zdnet.com/microsoft/?p=416, last accessed January 8, 2008.
77. www.microsoft-watch.com/article2/0,2180,1765128,00.asp, last accessed July 17, 2008.
78. Observers see in the launch of Live.com a pre-emptive move by Microsoft to head off an announcement of a similar initative by Google based on the OpenOffice open source suite (PCPRO.co.uk, November 10, 2005, last accessed July 17, 2008).
79. http://www.mozilla.org/about, last accessed July 17, 2008.
80. See www.mozilla.org/university/HOF.html, last accessed January 8, 2008, for an overview of vendors of Mozilla-related products.
81. IBM has in the past helped the Firefox browser team on its accessibility features. According to IBM officials, the company's developers built key pieces of accessibility code into the browser, including support for Microsoft Active Accessibility (MAA) (www.crn.com/sections/breakingnews/dailyarchives.jhtml?articleId=168600040, last accessed November 26, 2007).
82. www-306.ibm.com/able/news/firefox.html, last accessed July 17, 2008.
83. www.techworld.com/networking/news/index.cfm?NewsID=5115, last accessed July 17, 2008.
84. Soghoian, 2007. www.cnet.com/8301-13739_1-9776759-46.html?tag=blg.orig, A dangerous conflict of interest between Firefox and Google, last accessed January 8, 2008.
85. Magid, L., Mercurynews.com, November 5, 2007, www.mercurynews.com/business/ci_7374205, last accessed December 5, 2007.
86. Domingo, J.S. Foxnews, The laptop that could change the world, December 4, 2007. http://.www.foxnews.com/story/0,2933,314802,00.html, last accessed December 5, 2007.
87. Shankland. S. CNET.com, Mozilla aims Firefox at Mobile Devices. October 10, 2007. http://.www.news.com/8301-13580_3-9795028-39.html, last accessed November 26, 2007.
88. www.apple.com/safari, last accessed December 17, 2007.
89. http://netscape.aol.com/, last accessed February 12, 2008.
90. Barylick, C., Powerpage.org, November 2, 2007, www.powerpage.org/2007/11/netscape_x_902_firefox_2009_released.html, last accessed November 26, 2007.
91. Although there are no statistics available that differentiate between consumers and corporations, Firefox usage is higher at weekends than during the week (Sliwa, 2004), which suggests that its users consist primarily of consumers.
92. Interestingly, Gartner had advised clients to either strive for a "browser-agnostic" strategy or a multi-browser environment, to be better positioned

to take advantage of innovations, and ensure that their websites and applications do also run in a browser other than IE (Sliwa, 2006).

93. ADTECH usage share for Firefox, November 11, 2005, www.adtech.info/en/pr-05-10.html, last accessed July 17, 2008. Chapel. S., Firefox Cools Down, October 13, 2005, http://blogs.websidestory.com/datainsights/2005/09/firefox_cools_down_1.php, last accessed November 26, 2007. As of February 2006 the adoption rate in Europe is estimated at about 20% (Noon, 2006).

94. A recent survey by Computereconomics.com of what users consider the most important advantage of OSS indicated that IT decision makers value "reduced dependence on software vendors" as the most important advantage of OSS (Scavo, 2005).

95. Magid, L., Mercurynews.com, November 5, 2007, www.mercurynews.com/business/ci_7374205?nclick_check=1, last accessed December 5, 2007.

96. Domingo, J.S. Foxnews, The laptop that could change the world, December 4, 2007; www.foxnews.com/story/0,2933,314802,00.html, last accessed December 5, 2007.

97. Keizer, G., Linuxworld, Fix Firefox's memory problems, says Mozilla director, November 14, 2007, www.linuxworld.com.au/index.php/id;2067098313;fp;4;fpid;4, last accessed December 5, 2007.

98. Aughton. S., PCPro, 27 November, 2007, Mobile Firefox to debut on Windows Mobile, www.pcpro.co.uk/news/142083/mobile-firefox-to-debut-on-windows-mobile.html, last accessed December 5, 2007

99. Note that this is not about the development of the browser itself but just about the browser's roots.

100. Bishop, T., Firefox Beta 3 Released, November 20, 2007, http://blog.seattlepi.nwsource.com/microsoft/archives/126350.asp, last accessed November 27, 2007.

9   What can be Learnt from these Browser Wars

1. www.sourceforge.net, last accessed December 8, 2007.

2. Knowledge@Wharton, March 23, 2005, Will Firefox Burn Internet Explorer, http://knowledge.wharton.upenn.edu/ article.cfm?articleid=1162, last accessed July 17, 2008.

3. Foley, M.J., ZDNet, October 25, 2007, Up next: IE 8.0 http://blogs.zdnet.com/microsoft/?p=62, last accessed January 28, 2008.

4. Desmond, M, January 24, 2008, IE 8: Compliance Fix or House of Cards? http://reddevnews.com/blogs/weblog.aspx?blog=1852, last accessed January 28, 2008.

Appendix: Worldwide Market Share

1. Xiti Browsers Barometer (Xitigroup.com), 2007. Retrieved December 8, 2007 from www.xitimonitor.com/en-us/browsers-barometer/index-1-2-3-0.html

2. www.onestat.com/html/aboutus_pressbox53-firefox-mozilla-browser-market-share.html, last visited December 14, 2007.
3. Cheng, J. (2006) "Browser numbers released, IE still losing ground," Ars Technica, October 10, 2006, http://arstechnica.com/news.ars/post/20061010-7949.html, last accessed December 15, 2007.
4. www.e-janco.com/browser.htm, last accessed December 15, 2007; IT Productivity Center 2007; 2008.

References

Journals and papers

Anderson, P. and Tushman, M.L. (1990) "Technological discontinuities and dominant designs: a cyclical model of technological change," *Administrative Science Quarterly*, 35, pp. 604–633.

Antonelli, C. (1994) "Localized technological change and the evolution of standards as economics institutions," *Information Economics and Policy* 6 (3–4), pp. 195–216.

Arthur, W.B. (1989) "Competing technologies, increasing returns, and lock-in by historical events," *Economic Journal*, 97, pp. 642–665.

Arthur, W.B. (1996) "Increasing returns and the new world of business," *Harvard Business Review*, 74 (4), pp. 100–109.

Baker, S. (1998) "What every business should learn from Microsoft," *The Journal of Business Strategy*," 19 (5), p. 36.

Bekkers, R.N.A. (2001) *Mobile Telecommunication Standards: GSM, UMTS, TETRA and ERMES*, Boston: Artech House.

Besen, S.M. and Farrell, J. (1994) "Choosing how to compete: Strategies and tactics in standardization," *Journal of Economic Perspectives*, 8 (2), pp. 117–131.

Bitzer, J. and Schroder, P. (2004) "Competition and innovation in a technology setting software duopoly," DIW Discussion Papers, No. 363.

Bonaccorsi, A. and Rossi, C. (2003) "Why open source software can succeed," *Research Policy*, 32, pp. 1243–1258.

Bonaccorsi, A., Rossi, C., and Giannangeli, S. (2004) "Adaptive entry strategies under dominant standards – hybrid business models in the open source software industry," SSRN working paper, March 15, 2004.

Bresnahan, T.F. and Greenstein, S. (1999) "Technological competition and the structure of the computer industry," *Journal of Industrial Economics*, 47 (1), pp. 1–40.

Bresnahan, T.F. and Yin, P.-L. (2007) "Standard setting in markets: the browser war," in: Greensrein, S. and Stango, V. (eds) *Standards and Public Policy*, Cambridge: Cambridge University Press, pp. 18–60.

Casadesus-Masanell, R. and Ghemawat, P. (2006) "Dynamic mixed duopoly: a model motivated by Linux vs. Windows," *Management Science*, 52 (7), pp. 1072–1084.

Chandler, A. (1997) "The computer industry: the first half century," in: Yoffie, D.B. (ed.) *Competing in an Age of Digital Convergence*, Boston: Harvard Business School Press, pp. 37–122.

Church, J. and Gandal, N. (1992) "Network effects, software provision and standardization," *Journal of Industrial Economics*, 40 (1), pp. 85–104.

Corts, K.S. and Freier, D. (2003) "A brief history of the browser wars," *Harvard Business Case Study*, product nr 703517.

Crowston, K., Wei, K., Li, Q., Eseryel, U.Y., and Howison, J. (2005) "Coordination of free/libre open source software development," paper presented at the *International Conference on Information Systems*, Las Vegas.

Cushman, D.P. and Sanderson King. S. (2003) *Communication best practices at Dell, General Electric, Microsoft, and Monsanto*, Albany: State University of New York Press,.

Cusumano, M.A. (2004) "Reflections on Free and Open Software," *Communications of the ACM*, 47 (10), pp. 25–27.

Cusumano, M. and Selby, R. (1995) *Microsoft Secrets: How the World's Most Powerful Software Company Creates Technology, Shapes Markets, and Manages People*, New York: Free Press/Simon and Schuster.

Cusumano, M. and Yoffie, D. (1998) *Competing on Internet Time: Lessons from Netscape and Its Battle with Microsoft*, New York: Touchstone.

David, P. (1985) "Clio and the economy of QWERTY," *American Economic Review*, 75 (2), pp. 332–337.

De Vries, H.J. (1997) "Standardization – What's in a name?," *Terminology*, 4 (1) pp. 55–83 (Rectification in 4 (2)).

De Vries, H.J. (1998) "The Classification of Standards," *Knowledge Organization*, 25 (3), pp. 79–89.

De Vries, H.J. (1999) *Standardization – A Business Approach to the Role of National Standardization Organizations*, Boston/Dordrecht/London: Kluwer Academic Publishers, 341 pp.

De Vries, H.J. (2006) "Module 1: Fundamentals of Standards and standardization," in: Hesser, Feilzer, de Vries (eds), *Standardisation in Companies and Markets*, September 2006, Hamburg: Helmut Schmidt University Press, pp. 1–33.

De Vries, H.J. de, J.P.M. de Ruijter, and N. Argam (2007) "Dominant Design or Multiple Designs: The Flash Memory Card Case," in: Patrick Feng, Dan Meeking, and Richard Hawkins (eds) *Proceedings of the 5th International Conference on Standards and Innovation in Information Technology*. Piscataway, NJ: IEEE, pp. 12–22. (also on CD-ROM)

Dedrick, J. and West, J. (2004) "An Exploratory Study into Open Source Platform Adoption," *Proceedings of the 37th Annual Hawai'i International Conference on System Sciences*, Waikoloa, Hawaii (January 2004).

Economides, N. (1996) "The economics of networks," *International Journal of Industrial Organization*, 14 (6), pp. 669–890.

Economides, N. (1997) "Raising rivals' costs in complementary goods markets: LECs entering into long distance and Microsoft bundling Internet Explorer," Discussion Paper EC-98–03, New York: Stern School of Business.

Egyedi, T.M. and R. van Wendel de Joode (2004) "Standardization and other coordination mechanisms in open source software," *International Journal of IT Standards and Standardization Research*, 2 (1), pp. 1–17.

Ehrenhaft , D. (2001) *Marc Andreessen: Web Warrior*, Brookfield: Twenty-First Century Books.

Ehrhardt, M. (2004) "Network effects, standardization and competitive strategy: how companies influence the emergence of dominant designs," *International Journal of Technology Management*, 27 (2/3), pp. 272–294.

Farrell, J. and Gallini, N. (1988) "Second-sourcing as a commitment: monopoly incentives to attract competition," *Quarterly Journal of Economics*, 103 (4), pp. 673–694.

Farrell J., Saloner, G. (1985) "Standardization, compatibility, and innovation," *Rand Journal*, 16, pp. 70–83.

Farrell, J. and Saloner, G. (1986) "Installed Base and Compatibility: Innovation, Product Preannouncements, and Predation," *The American Economic Review*, 76 (5), pp. 940–955.

Farrell, J. and Saloner, G. (1988) "Coordination through committees and markets," *Rand Journal of Economics* 19 (2), pp. 235–252.

Fink, M. (2003) *The Business and Economics of Linux and Open Source*, Upper Saddle River, NJ: Prentice Hall PTR.

Fitzgerald, B., Feller, J., Hissam, S.A., and Lakhani, K.R. (2005) *Perspectives on Free and Open Source Software*, Cambridge, MA: MIT Press.

Frost, J.J. (2005) "Some economic and legal aspects of open source software," paper University of Washington Department of Economics.

Fuggetta, A. (2003) "Open source software – an evaluation," *The Journal of Systems and Software*, 66, pp. 77–90.

Gallagher, S. (2007) "The complementary role of dominant designs and industry standards," *IEEE Transactions on Engineering Management*, 54 (2), pp. 371–379.

Garud, R. and Kumaraswamy, A. (1993) "Changing competitive dynamic in network industries: an exploration of Sun Microsystem's open systems strategy," *Strategic Management Journal*, 14, pp. 351–369.

Ghosh, R., Glott, R., Krieger B., and Robles, G. (2002) "Survey of developers, free/libre and open source software: survey and study, FLOSS, final report," International Institute of Infonomics, Berlecom Research GmbH.

Gilbert, R.J. and Katz, M.L. (2001) "An economist's guide to U.S. v. Microsoft," *Journal of Economic Perspectives,* Spring issue 2001, 15, pp. 25–44.

Gove, B. (1993) "Webster's Third New International Dictionary of the English Language Unabridged," Könemann, Cologne, Germany.

Grant, R.M. (2002) *Contemporary Strategy Analysis*, 4th edition, Massachussets: Blackwell publishing Ltd.

Grindley, P. (1992) *Standards, Business Strategy and Policy: A Casebook*, London: London Business School.

Grindley, P. (1995) *Standards, Strategy and Policy: Cases and Stories*, Oxford: Oxford University Press.

Gupta, V., Gollakota, K., and Srinivasan, R. (2005) *Business Policy and Strategic Management – Concepts and Applications*, India: Prentice Hall of India Pvt.Ltd.

Haigh, T. (2002) "Software in the 1960s as concept, service, and product," *IEEE Annals of the History of Computing*, 24 (1) 2002, pp. 5–13.

Hax, A.C. and Wilde, D.L. (1999) "The Delta Model: adaptive management for a changing world," *Sloan Management Review,* 40 (2), pp. 11–28.

Hax, A.C. (2002) "Achieving the potentials of your organization – how to overcome the dangers of commoditization," working paper 4260–02, MIT Sloan School of Management, https://dspace.mit.edu/bitstream/

1721.1/1854/2/4260-02.pdf, September 2002. Last accessed on November 14, 2007.

Hayashi, K. (1992) "From network externalities to interconnection: the changing nature of networks and economy" in: Antonelli, C. (ed.) *The Economics of Information Networks*, Massachussets: Elsevier Science Publishers B.V., pp. 195–215.

Hoch, D.J., Roeding, C., Lindner, S.K., and Purkert, G. (2000) *Secrets of Software Success: Management Insights from 100 Software Firms around the World*, Boston: Harvard Business School Press.

ISO (2004) "ISO 8601:2004 – Data elements and interchange formats – information interchange – representation of dates and times," 3rd ed. Geneva: International Organization for Standardization.

IT Productivity Center (2007) *Browser & OS Market Share White Paper September 2007*. Park City, UT: Janco Associates Inc.

IT Productivity Center (2008) *Browser & OS Market Share White Paper April 2008*. Park City, UT: Janco Associates Inc.

Jenkins, M., Liu, P., Matzkin, R.L., and McFadden, D.L. (2004) "The browser war – econometric analysis of markov perfect equilibrium in markets with network effects," working paper, Berkeley: University of California.

Katz, M.L. and Shapiro, C. (1985) "Network externalities, competition, and compatibility," *American Economic Review*, 75 (3), pp. 424–440.

Katz, M.L. and Shapiro, C. (1986) "Technology adoption in the presence of network externalities," *Journal of Political Economy*, 94 (4), pp. 822–841.

Katz, M.L. and Shapiro, C. (1992) "Product introduction with network externalities," *Journal of Industrial Economics*, XL (1), pp. 55–84.

Katz, M.L. and Shapiro, C. (1994) "Systems competition and network effects," *Journal of Economic Perspectives*, 8 (2) (Spring, 1994), pp. 93–115.

Katz, M.L. and Shapiro, C. (1998) "Antitrust in Software Markets," Working paper, Berkeley, CA: University of California at Berkeley.

Kenwood, C.A. (2001) "A business case study of open source software," paper, Massachussets, MITRE Corporation.

Klein, B. (2001) "The Microsoft case: what can a dominant firm to defend its market position?," *Journal of Economic Perspectives*, 15 (2), pp. 45–62.

Klemperer, P. (1987) "The Competitiveness of Markets with Switching Costs," *The RAND Journal of Economics*, 18 (1) (Spring, 1987), pp. 138–150.

Knowledge @ Wharton (2005) "Browser Wars: will Firefox burn Explorer?," March 23, 2005, http://knowledge.wharton.upenn.edu/article/1162.cfm, last accessed on November 14, 2007.

Kogut, B., Metiu, A. (2001) "Open-source software development and distributed innovation," *Oxford Review of Economic Policy*, 2, pp. 248–264.

Krechmer, K. (2002) "Cathedrals, Libraries and Bazaards," Paper presented at the Association of Computing Machinery (ACM) Symposium on Applied Computing SAC 2002, March 10–13, 2002, Madrid, Spain. http://www.csrstds.com/cathedrals.html, last accessed July 17, 2008.

Krechmer, K. (2006) "Open standards requirements," *International Journal of IT standards and Standardization Research*, 4 (1), pp. 43–61.

Krishnamurthy, S. (2002) "Page: 7 cave or community? An empirical examination of 100 mature open source projects," May 2002, http://opensource.mit.edu/papers/krishnamurthy.pdf, last accessed on November 14, 2007.

Krishnamurthy, S. (2003) "An analysis of open source business models," Forthcoming in: Joseph Feller, Brian Fitzgerald, Scott Hissam, and Karim Lakhani (eds) *Making Sense of the Bazaar: Perspectives on Open Source and Free Software*, Boston: MIT Press, pp. 279–297.

Krishnamurthy, S. (2005a) "About closed-door free/*libre*/open Source (FLOSS) projects: lessons from the Mozilla Firefox developer recruitment," *UPGRADE*, VI (3), pp. 1–21.

Krishnamurthy, S. (2005b) "The launching of Mozilla Firefox – a case study in community-led marketing," working paper, available at http://opensource.mit.edu/papers/sandeep2.pdf, last accessed on July 19, 2008.

Lerner, J. and Tirole, J. (2004) "The economics of technology sharing: open source and beyond," NBER working paper No. 10956, National Bureau of Economic Research, December 2004, Harvard NOM Working Series.

Lerner, J. and Tirole, J. (2000) "The simple economics of open source," NBER working paper No. 7600, Cambridge, MA: Harvard University.

Liebowitz, S.J. and Margolis (1990) "The fable of the keys," *Journal of Law and Economics*, 33 (1), pp. 1–26.

Liebowitz, S.J. and Margolis, S.E. (1996) "Market processes and the selection of standards," *Harvard Journal of Law and Technology*, 9, pp. 283–318.

MacCormack, A., Rusnak, J., and Baldwin, C.Y. (2004) "Exploring the structure of complex software designs: an empirical study of open source and proprietary code," Harvard Business School Working Paper Series, No. 05–016, 2004, Harvard Business School, Harvard Press.

McKinsey and Company (1999) *NASSCOM McKinsey Study: Indian I.T. Strategies*, New Delhi: NASSCOM.

Majamar, S. and Venktaraman, S. (1998) "Network effects and the adoption of new technology: evidence from the US telecommunications industry," *Strategic Management Journal*, 19, pp. 1045–1062.

Mann, R.J. (2004) "The myth of the software patent thicket," American Law and Economics Association Annual Meeting 2004, Paper 44, Califorina, The Berkeley Electronic Press.

Mendonca, L.T. and Sutton, R. (2008) "Succeeding at open-source innovation: An interview with Mozilla's Mitchell Baker," *McKinsey Quarterly*, January 2008, www.ciozone.com, last accessed on July 20, 2008.

Mendys-Kamphorst, E. (2002) "Open vs. Closed: some consequences of the open source movement for software markets," CPB Discussion Paper, no. 13.

Meng, Z. and Lee, S.Y.T (2005) "Open Source vs. Proprietary Software: competition and compatibility," Industrial Organization, Paper No. 0508009, August 10, 2005.

Mockus, A., R.T. Fielding, and H.D. Herbsleb (2002) "Two case studies of open source software development: Apache and Mozilla," *ACM Transactions on Software Engineering and Methodology*, 11(3), pp. 309–346.

Morrison, S., Waters, R. (2005) "Battle of the browsers is set to be replayed," *Financial Times*, p. 13, August 5, 2005. http://search.ft.com/ftArticle?query Text=Battle+of+the+browsers+is+set+to+be+replayed&aje=true&id=05080 5000599&ct=0&nclick_check=1, last accessed on November 14, 2007.

Nalebuff, B.J. and Brandenburger, A.M. (1997) "Co-opetition: competitive and cooperative business strategies for the digital economy," *Strategy and Leadership*, 25 (6), p. 28.

Newman, N. (1997) "How Netscape stole the web, or destroying the village in order to save it," www.xent.com/FoRK-archive/winter96/0667.html, last accessed on July 20, 2008.

Nuttall, C. (2005) "Companies international: Microsoft extends openness software," *Financial Times*, September 20, 2004, http://search.ft.com/ftArti cle?queryText=Microsoft+extends+openness+softwareandy=0andaje=true andx=0andid=040920000949andct=0, last accessed on November 15, 2007.

Oshri, I. and Weeber, C. (2006) "Cooperation and competition standards-setting activities in the digitization era: the case of wireless information devices," *Technology Analysis and Strategic Management*, 8 (2), pp. 265–283.

Rohlfs, J. (1974) "A theory of interdependent demand for a communications service," *Bell Journal of Economics*, 5 (1), pp. 16–37.

Scacchi, W., Feller, J., Fitzgerald, B., Hissam, S., and Lakhani, K. (2006) "Guest editorial: understanding free/open source software development processes," *Software Process Improvement and Practice*, 11, pp. 95–105.

Sebenius, J.K. (2002) "Negotiating lessons from the browser wars," *MIT Sloan Management Review*, 43 (4), pp. 43–50.

Shapiro, C. and Varian, H.R. (1999a) "The art of standard wars," *California Management Review*, 41 (2), p. 8.

Shapiro, C. and Varian, H.R. (1999b) *Information Rules: A Strategic Guide to the Networked Economy*, Boston: Harvard Business School Press.

Silverthorne, S. (2005) "Microsoft vs. Open Source: who will win?," *HBS Working Knowledge*, June 6, 2005, http://hbswk.hbs.edu/item.jhtml?id=4834 andt=technology, last accessed on November 14, 2007.

Simons, C.A.J. and De Vries, H.J. (2002) *Standaardisatie en Normalisatie. Deel 3: Innovatie en bedrijfsnormalisatie*, Engineering Dossiers, The Hague: Ten Hagen and Stam B.V.

Spinellis, D. and Szyperski, C. (2004) "How is open source affecting software development?," *IEEE Software*, 21 (1), pp. 28–33.

Stango, V. (2004) "The economics of standard wars," *Review of Network Economics*, 3 (1), pp. 1–19.

Suarez, F.F. and Utterback, J.M. (1995) "Dominant designs and the survival of firms," *Strategic Management Journal*, 16 (6), pp. 415–430.

Succi, G., Predonzeni, P., Valerio, A., and Vernazza, T. (1998) "Representing compatibility and standards: a case study of web browsers,"*ACM StandardView*, 6 (2), pp. 69–75.

Van der Kaa, G. (2005) "Standardization in complex systems," PhD research proposal RSM Erasmus University, dated February 8, 2006.

Van Wegberg, M. (2004) "Standardization process of systems technologies: creating a balance between competition and cooperation," *Technology Analysis and Strategic Management*, 16 (4), pp. 457–478.

von Hippel, E. and von Krogh, G. (2003) "Open source software and the private-collective innovation model: Issues for organization science," *Organization Science*, 14 (2), pp. 209–223.

Von Krogh, G. and Hippel, von. E (2003) "Editorial, special issue on open source software development," *Research Policy*, 32, pp. 1149–1157.

Walker, D.A. (2001) "A popular monopoly: United States v. Microsoft," in John W. Johnson (ed.), *Historic U.S. Court Cases*, New York, NY: Routledge, pp. 402–408.

Wang, T., Wu, L., and Lin, Z. (2005) "The Revival of Mozilla in the Browser War against Internet Explorer," ICEC'05 Xi'an China, August 15–17, 2005.

Weiss, M.B.H. and Spring, M.B. (1992) "Selected Intellectual Property Issues in Standardization," paper presented at the *Twentieth Annual Telecommunications Policy Research Conference*, Solomons, MD, September 12–14, 1992.

West, J. (2003a) "How open is open enough? Melding proprietary and open source platform strategies," *Research Policy*, 32, pp. 1259–1285.

West, J. (2003b) "The Role of Standards in the Creation and Use of Information Systems," paper presented at *Standard Making; A Critical Research Frontier for Information Systems*, MISQ special issue workshop, December 14, 2003, Seattle, USA.

West, J. (2004) "What Are Open Standards? Implications for Adoption, Competition and Policy," paper presented at *Standards and Public Policy conference*, Federal Reserve Bank of Chicago, May 13, 2004.

West, J. and Dedrick, J. (2001) "Open source standardization: the rise of Linux in the network era," *Knowledge, Technology and Policy*, 14 (2), pp. 88–112.

West, J. and Gallagher, S. (2004) "Key challenges of open innovation: lessons from open source software," working paper, May 31, 2004, available at http://www.cob.sjsu.edu/west_j/Papers/WestGallagher2004.pdf, last accessed on July 21, 2008.

Wichmann, T. (2002) "Firms' open source activities: motivations and policy implications. free/libre and open source software," FLOSS Final Report, International Institute of Infonomics, Berlecom Research GmbH.

Williams, S. (2002) "Free as in freedom: Richard Stallman's crusade for free software," Cambridge, MA, O'Reilly.

Windrum, P. (1999) "Back from the brink: Microsoft and the strategic use of standards in the browser wars," *Communication to European Meeting on Applied Evolutionary Economics*, June 7–9, 1999, http://web.upmf-grenoble.fr/iepe/textes/windrum.PDF, last accessed on November 14, 2007.

Windrum, P. (2000) "Back from the brink: Microsoft and the strategic use of standards in the Browser Wars," Research Memoranda number 005, Maastricht : MERIT, Maastricht Economic Research Institute on Innovation and Technology.

Windrum, P. (2004) "Leveraging technological externalities in complex technologies: Microsoft's exploitation of standards in the browser wars," *Research Policy*, 33, pp. 385–394.

World Bank (2005) *Open Source Software: Perspectives on Development*, Valencia: Press Group Holdings Europe.

Yoffie, D.B. and Cusumano, M.A. (1999) "Building a company on Internet time: Lessons from Netscape," *California Management Review*, 41 (3), pp. 8.

Yoffie, D.B. and Cusumano, M.A. (1999) "Judo strategy. The competitive dynamics of Internet time," *Harvard Business Review*, 77 (1), pp. 70–81.

Yoffie, D.B. and Kwak, M. (2001) "The browser wars, 1994–1998," published June 1998, revised January 22, 2001, *Harvard Business School Case*.

Newspapers

Andrews, P. (1997) "Two years ago Gates dropped a Warhead that is still exploding," *Seattle Times*, December 07, 1997, http://community.seattletimes.nwsource.com/archive/?date=19971207&slug=2576751, last accessed on July 21, 2008.

Arstechnica (2004) "Firefox hits the big 1.0," November 09, 2004, http://arstechnica.com/news.ars/post/20041109-4387.html, last accessed on November 14, 2007.

Baker, M. (2004) "The Mozilla project and mozilla.org," on www.mozilla.org/editorials/mozilla-overview.html, last accessed on November 14, 2007.

BBC com (2004) "Firefox browser takes on Microsoft," November 09, 2004, http://news.bbc.co.uk/1/hi/technology/3993959.stm, last accessed on November 14, 2007.

BBC.com (2005) "The assault on software giant Microsoft," May 09, 2005, http://news.bbc.co.uk/1/hi/business/4508897.stm. last accessed on November 14, 2007.

BBC.com (2005)"How Microsoft plans to beat its rivals," May 10, 2005, http://news.bbc.co.uk/1/hi/business/4516269.stm, last accessed on November 14, 2007.

Bray, H. (2005) "Opera to give away browser in bid to boost market share," *Boston Globe*, September 20, 2005, www.boston.com/business/technology/articles/2005/09/20/opera_to_give_away_browser_in_bid_to_boost_market_share/, last accessed on November 14, 2007.

Broersma, M. (2005a) "Intel bets on open source future," *ZDNet* UK, August 08, 2005, http://news.zdnet.co.uk/hardware/0,1000000091,39212453,00.htm, last accessed on November 14, 2007.

Broersma, M. (2005b) "Browser wars: Episode II," *ZDNet* UK, February 28, 2005, http://insight.zdnet.co.uk/internet/security/0,39020457,39189477,00.htm, last accessed on November 14, 2007.

Cheng, J. (2006). "Browser numbers released, IE still losing ground," *Ars Technica*, October 10, 2006, http://arstechnica.com/news.ars/post/20061010-7949.html, last accessed on December 15, 2007.

Chakraborty, A. (2004) "The fox is in Microsoft's henhouse (and salivating)," *The New York Times*, December 19, 2004.

Corcoran, E. (2004) "Bill Grows Up," *Forbes*, April 10, 2004, www.forbes.com/ philanthropy/2004/10/04/cz_ec_1004gates.html, last accessed on November 14 2007.

Cornell University, http://iws.cit.cornell.edu/iws2/technology/techinfo.cfm, last accessed on November 16, 2007.

Costa, D., CNET Editor's Choice (2004), http://reviews.cnet.com/browsers/ mozilla-firefox/4505-3514_7-31117280.html, last accessed January 8, 2008.

Eggheaddesign.co.uk, www.eggheaddesign.co.uk/glossary.aspx, last accessed on November 16, 2007.

eWeek.com (2003) "Microsoft warns SEC of open-source threat," February 03, 2003, www.eweek.com/article2/0,3959,857638,00.asp, last accessed on November 14, 2007.

Festa, P., CNET News (2004) "Browsers: a return to arms," part of *The year in review*, December, 2004, http://news.com.com/Year+in+review+Browser+ wars,+part+2/2009-1032_3-5495797.html, last accessed on November 15, 2007.

Financial Times (2005) "Time is right for Mozilla switch," September 21, 2005, p. 3.

Foley, M.J. (2004) "Microsoft releases source code on SourceForge," *Microsoft-Watch.com*, April 05, 2004, www.microsoft-watch.com/content/operating_ systems/microsoft_releases_source_code_on_sourceforge.html, last accessed on November 14, 2007.

Forbes (2005) "Firefox goes for-profit," August 3, 2005, www.forbes.com/ business/2005/08/03/mozilla-firefox-forprofit-cx_ld_0803mozilla.html, last accessed on November 14, 2007.

Greene, J. (2005) "Opening new Windows on the Web," *Business Week*, November 14, 2005, p. 21.

Lohr, S. and Markoff, J. (2004) "In the battle of the browsers '04, Firefox aims at Microsoft," *New York Times*, November 15, 2004, www.nytimes. com/2004/11/15/technology/15browser.html, last accessed on November 14, 2007.

Marson, I. (2005) "Firefox sneaks into the enterprise," *ZDNet* UK, March 01, 2005, http://news.zdnet.co.uk/software/applications/0,39020384,3918958 5,00.htm, last accessed on November 14, 2007.

McHugh, J. (2005) "The Firefox explosion," *Wired Magazine*, issue 13.02, www.wired.com/wired/archive/13.02/firefox.html?pg=2andtopic=firefoxa ndtopic_set, last accessed on November 14, 2007.

Microsoft, http://msdn2.microsoft.com/en-us/library/ms970422.aspx, last accessed on November 16, 2007.

Morrison, S. (2004) "Firefox uses cunning to take on the Godzilla of Microsoft," *Financial Times*, p. 20, November 8, 2004.

Mossberg, W.S. (2004) "Security, cool features of Firefox Web Browser beat Microsoft's IE," December 30, 2004, http://armwoodtechnology.blogspot. com/2004_12_26_archive.html, last accessed on November 14, 2007.

Mozilla.org, www.mozilla.org/MPL/NPL-1.1.html, last accessed on November 16, 2007.

Mozilla.org, http://developer.mozilla.org/en/docs/Glossary, last accessed on November 16, 2007.

MSDN Ieblog (2006) http://blogs.msdn.com/ie/archive/2006/08/22/712830. aspx, last accessed on November 16, 2007.

Netscape Press Release (1998) "Netscape launches aggressive 'unlimited distribution' program for new free client software," January 22, 1998, http://wp.netscape.com/newsref/pr/newsrelease560.html. last accessed on November 14, 2007.

Noon, C. (2006) "French police abandon Ballmer's Microsoft for Mozilla," *Forbes*, February 06, 2006, www.forbes.com/facesinthenews/2006/02/06/ballmer-microsoft-france-cx_cn_0206autofacescan03.html?partner=rss, last accessed on November 14, 2007.

Nuttall, C. (2005) "Manner of the web: start-ups map the route as big rivals get Microsoft in their sights," *Financial Times*, November 17, 2005, www.ft.com/cms/s/0/9b5f7616-570e-11da-b98c-00000e25118c.html, last accessed on November 15, 2007.

OneStat Press Release (2005) "Mozilla's browsers global usage share is still growing according to OneStat.com," November 02, 2005, www.onestat.com/html/aboutus_pressbox40_browser_market_firefox_growing.html

Paul, R. (2007) "First look: Safari 3 beta on Windows vs. Firefox 2 and IE7." *Ars Technica*, June 12, 2007. http://arstechnica.com/news.ars/post/20070612-afirst-look-safari-3-on-windows.html, last accessed on December 15, 2007.

PC World (2005) "Are fewer people switching to Firefox?," March 01, 2005, www.pcworld.com/news/article/0,aid,119849,00.asp, last accessed on November 15, 2007.

Vamosi, R., PC Mag.com, "Review Firefox 2.0," http://reviews.cnet.com/browsers/firefox-2/4505-3514_7-32126746.html?tag=pm, last accessed on January 08, 2008.

PCPRO UK (2005) "Microsoft's Live.com supports Firefox," November 10, 2005, www.pcpro.co.uk/news/79703/microsofts-livecom-supports-firefox.html, last accessed on November 15, 2007.

Pegoraro, R. (2004) "Firefox leaves no reason to endure Internet Explorer," November 14, 2004, www.washingtonpost.com/wp-dyn/articles/A47146-2004Nov13.html, last accessed on November 15, 2007.

Penfield Jackson, T. (1999) "Finding of fact in US v. Microsoft," November 09, 1999, www.usdoj.gov/atr/cases/f3800/msjudgex.htm, last accessed on November 15, 2007.

Perez, G.C. (2005) "Firefox faces challenges as it matures," *InfoWorld*, September 20, 2005, www.infoworld.com/article/05/09/20/HNfirefoxmatures_1.html, last accessed on November 15, 2007.

Perez, J.C. (2005) "Firefox still chipping away at IE," *PCWorld*, June 13, 2005 www.pcworld.com/resource/article/0,aid,121362,pg,1,RSS,RSS,00.asp, last accessed on November 15, 2007.

Rapoza, J. (2004) "Firefox 1.0 lives up to hype," *eWeek*, November 09, 2004, www.eweek.com/article2/0,1895,1722370,00.asp, last accessed on May 11, 2006.

Raymond, E.S (1998a) "Goodbye, 'free software'; hello, 'open source'," February 08, 1998, www.catb.org/~esr/open-source.html, last accessed on November 15, 2007.

Raymond, E.S. (1998b) "The Halloween papers," November 25, 1998, www.opensource.org/halloween/, last accessed on November 15, 2007.

Ross, B. (2005) "Developer recruitment in Firefox," January 25, 2005, http://64.233.169.104/search?q=cache:bBLQfF8Mx70J:blakeross.com/index.php%3Fp%3D19+Developer+recruitment+in+Firefoxandhl=enandc t=clnkandcd=1andclient=firefox-a, last accessed on November 15, 2007.

Scavo, F. (2005) "Key advantage of open source is not cost savings," May 12, 2005, www.computereconomics.com/article.cfm?id=1043, last accessed on November 15, 2007.

Searchwindevelopment.com, http://searchwindevelopment.techtarget.com/sDefinition/0,,sid8_gci211708,00.html, last accessed on November 16, 2007.

Shankland, S. (2005) "FAQ: the Sun-Google partnership," October 04, 2005, http://news.com.com/FAQ+The+Sun-Google+partnership/2100-1012_3-5888783.html?tag=nl, last accessed on November 15, 2007.

Shankland, S. (2007), "Mozilla aims Firefox at Mobile Devices," October 10, 2007, http://www.news.com/8301-13580_3-9795028-39.html, last accessed November 26, 2007.

Sliwa, C. (2004) "Who's using Firefox," *ComputerWorld*, November 29, 2004, www.pcworld.com/article/id,118729-page,1/article.html, last accessed on November 15, 2007.

Sliwa, C. (2006) "Firefox finds cracking the corporate market a challenge," *Computerworld*, February 16, 2006, www.computerworld.com/softwaretopics/software/story/0,10801,108622p3,00.html, last accessed on November 15, 2007.

Softpedia News (2005) "Mozilla wants to make some cash," August 03, 2005, http://news.softpedia.com/news/Mozilla-Wants-to-Make-Some-Cash-5828.shtml, last accessed on November 15, 2007.

Taylor, P. (2004) "Technology: browsing through the browser options," *Financial Times*, October 06, 2004, http://search.ft.com/ftArticle?queryText= Browsing+through+the+browser+optionsandy=11andaje=trueandx=21and id=041006001065andct=0, last accessed on November 15, 2007.

Taylor, P (2005) "Business life sciences and technology: better manners to be an explorer on the internet," *Financial Times*, November 02, 2005, http://search.ft.com/ftArticle?queryText=Better+manners+to+be+an+explorer+on+the+internetandy=7andaje=falseandx=15andid=051202001264andct=0, last accessed on November 15, 2007.

Thurrott, P. (1999) "Microsoft lawyers, professor spar over Web browser definition," May 26, 1999, www.windowsitpro.com/Article/ArticleID/18710/18710.html, last accessed on November 15, 2007.

Valloppillil, V. (1998) http://opensource.feratech.com/halloween/halloween1.php, last accessed on November 26, 2007.

W3Schools.com, www.w3schools.com/browsers/browsers_stats.asp, last accessed on November 16, 2007.

Waters, R. (2005) "Comment and analysis: obstacles stand in the manner of a cultural shift," *Financial Times*, November 17, 2005, http://search.ft.com/ftArticle?queryText=Obstacles+stand+in+the+manner+of+a+cultural+shift andy=11andaje=trueandx=13andid=051117000991andct=0, last accessed on November 15, 2007.

Zawinski, J. (1999) "Resignation and postmortem," March 31, 1999, www.jwz.org/gruntle/nomo.html, last accessed on November 15, 2007.

ZDNet Australia (2004) "Microsoft: Firefox does not threaten IE's market share," November 11, 2004, www.zdnet.com.au/news/ 0,39023165,39166227,00.htm, last accessed on November 15, 2007.

ZDNet News (2004) "New Netscape embraces Firefox, IE," November 30, 2004, http://news.zdnet.com/2100-9588_22-5470378.html, last accessed on November 15, 2007.

ZDNet UK (2005) "Firefox 1.5 'smashes' 1.0 download stats," December 01, 2005, http://news.zdnet.co.uk/software/applications/0,39020384,3923930 3,00.htm, last accessed on November 15, 2007.

CNET.com

CNET News (1998) "Microsoft spins 'Halloween' memos," November 06, 1998, http://news.com.com/Microsoft+spins+Halloween+memos/2100-1001_3-217647.html, , last accessed on November 15, 2007.

CNET News (1998) "New engine for Mozilla code," April 16, 1998, http://news.com.com/2100-1001-210279.html, last accessed on November 15, 2007.

CNET News (2002) "AOL's Netscape sues Microsoft," January 22, 2002, http://news.com.com/2100-1001-820227.html, last accessed on November 15, 2007.

CNET News.com (2003) "AOL lays off Netscape developers," July 15, 2003, http://news.com.com/AOL+lays+off+Netscape+developers/2100-1032_3-1026078.html, last accessed on November 15, 2007.

CNET News (2003) "Apple snub stings Mozilla," January 14, 2003, http://news.com.com/Apple+snub+stings+Mozilla/2100-1023_3-980492.html?tag=nl, last accessed on November 15, 2007.

CNET News (2003) "Developers gripe about IE standards inaction," October 09, 2003, http://news.com.com/2100-1032_3-5088642.html, last accessed on November 15, 2007.

CNET News (2003) "Microsoft to pay AOL $750 million", May 29, 2003, http://news.com.com/Microsoft+to+pay+AOL+750+million/2100-1032_3-1011296.html?tag=nl, last accessed on November 15, 2007.

CNET News (2003) "Phoenix rises from Mozilla's ashes," April 02, 2003, http://news.com.com/Phoenix+rises+from+Mozillas+ashes/2100-1025_3-995251.html?tag=nl, last accessed on November 15, 2007.

CNET News (2003) "W3C releases scripting standard, caveat," January 09, 2003, http://news.com.com/2100-1023-979976.html, last accessed on November 15, 2007.

CNET News (2003) "With update, Mozilla introduces fees," October 15, 2003, http://news.com.com/2100-1032-5091869.html, last accessed on November 15, 2007.

CNET News (2004) "Google stars in Firefox's new browser," November 11, 2004, http://news.com.com/Google+stars+in+Firefoxs+new+browser/210 0-1032_3-5449172.html, last accessed on November 15, 2007.

CNET News (2004) "Newsmaker: unearthing the origins of Firefox," October 13, 2004, http://news.com.com/Unearthing+the+origins+of+Firefox/200 8-1032_3-5406708.html, last accessed on November 15, 2007.

CNET News (2004) "Nokia cash boosts Mozilla," June 18, 2004, http://news. com.com/Nokia+cash+boosts+Mozilla/2100-7344_3-5236730.html? tag=nl, last accessed on November 15, 2007.

CNET News (2004) "Move over, Internet Explorer," November 10, 2004, updated on March 24, 2005, http://reviews.cnet.com/Mozilla_Firefox/ 4505-9241_7-31117280.html, last accessed on November 15, 2007.

CNET News (2005) "A standards truce in the browser war?," August 04, 2005, http://news.com.com/A+standards+truce+in+the+browser+war/2100-1013_3-5818382.html, last accessed on November 15, 2007.

CNET News (2005) "Firefox plans mass marketing drive," November 26, 2005, http://news.com.com/Firefox+plans+mass+marketing+drive/2100-7344_3-5972089.html?tag=nefd.top, last accessed on November 15, 2007.

CNET News (2005) "Google introduces ad-services referral program," November 07, 2005, http://news.com.com/Google+introduces+ad-services+referral+program/2100-1024_3-5937844.html, last accessed on November 15, 2007.

CNET News (2005) "IBM backs Firefox in-house," May 12, 2005, http://news. com.com/IBM+backs+Firefox+in-house/2100-7344_3-5704750.html, last accessed on November 15, 2007.

CNET News (2005) "IBM updates Linux desktop with Firefox support," August 09, 2005, www.news.com/IBM-updates-Linux-desktop-with-Firefox-support/2100-1012_3-5825739.html, last accessed on November 15, 2007.

CNET News (2005) "Unpatched Firefox 1.5 exploit made public," December 08, 2005, http://news.com.com/Unpatched+Firefox+1.5+exploit+made+public/2100-1002_3-5987401.html?tag=html.alert, last accessed on November 15, 2007.

CNET News (2005) "Firefox downloaded 75 million times," July 26, 2005, http://news.com.com/Firefox+downloaded+75+million+times/2100-1032_3-5805807.html, last accessed on November 15, 2007.

CNET News. (2005) "Fix in for Firefox bugs," September 21, 2005, http:// news.com.com/Fix+in+for+Firefox+bugs/2100-1002_3-5875797.html? tag=nl, last accessed on November 15, 2007.

Mozilla.com/org

www.mozilla.com/en-US/firefox/2.0.0.9/releasenotes/, last accessed at November 26, 2007 www.mozilla.com/press/mozilla-2005-12-2.html, last accessed on November 15, 2007.

www.mozilla.org, last accessed on November 15, 2007.

www.mozilla.org/about, last accessed on November 15, 2007.

www.mozilla.org/about/fast-facts, last accessed on July 17, 2008.

www.mozilla.org/about/timeline, last accessed on November 15, 2007.

www.mozilla.org/credits/, last accessed January 8, 2008.

www.mozilla.org/foundation/trademarks/policy.html, last accessed on November 15, 2007.

www.mozilla.org/hacking/code-review-faq.html, last accessed on July 17, 2008.

www.mozilla.org/hacking/reviewers.html, Eich, B. and Baker, M. Mozilla "super-review," last accessed January 8, 2008.

www.mozilla.org/mission.html, last accessed on November 15, 2007.

www.mozilla.org/MPL, last accessed November 26, 2007.

www.mozilla.org/MPL/FAQ.html#7, last accessed at November 26, 2007.

www.mozilla.org/MPL/license-policy.html, last accessed November 26, 2007.

www.mozilla.org/MPL/MPL-1.1.html, last accessed on November 15, 2007.

www.mozilla.org/MPL/relicensing-faq.html, last accessed on November 15, 2007.

www.mozilla.org/newlayout/faq.html, last accessed on July 17, 2008.

www.mozilla.org/newlayout; last accessed on November 15, 2007.

www.mozilla.org/owners.html, last accessed on July 17, 2008.

www.mozilla.org/press/mozilla-2005-08-03.html, last accessed November 15, 2007.

www.mozilla.org/projects/firefox/charter.html, last accessed on July 17, 2008.

www.mozilla.org/reorganization/, last accessed on July 17, 2008.

www.mozilla.org/roadmap/roadmap-26-Oct-1998.html, last accessed on July 17, 2008.

www.mozilla.org/support/firefox/faq#free, last accessed on July 17, 2008.

www.mozillazine.org/talkback.html?article=4155, last accessed on November 15, 2007.

www.mozillazine.org/talkback.html?article=6203, last accessed on July 17, 2008.

www.mozillazine.org/talkback.html?article=6900, last accessed on July 17, 2008.

https://addons.mozilla.org/?application=firefox, last accessed on January 8, 2008.

Websites: miscellaneous

"ADTECH usage share for Firefox," November 11, 2005 www.adtech.info/en/pr-05-10.html, last accessed July 17, 2008.

Aughton. S., PCPro, "Mobile Firefox to debut on Windows Mobile," November 27, 2007, www.pcpro.co.uk/news/142083/mobile-firefox-to-debut-on-windows-mobile.html, last accessed on December 05, 2007

Barylick, C., Powerpage.org, November 02, 2007, www.powerpage. org/2007/11/netscape_x_902_firefox_2009_released.html, last accessed November 26, 2007.

BBC News, "Microsoft loses anti-trust appeal," September 17, 2007, http:// news.bbc.co.uk/2/hi/business/6998272.stm, last accessed November 26, 2007.

Berners-Lee T. and Fischetti M. (2000) *Weaving the Web the Original Design and Ultimate Destiny of the World Wide Web*, New York: Collins.

Bishop, T. "Firefox Beta 3 released," November 20, 2007, http://blog.seattlepi. nwsource.com/microsoft/archives/126350.asp, last accessed November 27, 2007.

Cabello, P. Mozillalinks, "Next steps for Firefox," November 24, 2007, http:// mozillalinks.org/wp/2007/11/next-steps-for-firefox-3/, last accessed on December 08, 2007.

Cailliau, R. "A little history on the world wide web," www.w3.org/History. htm, last accessed December 08, 2007,

Chapel. S. "Firefox cools down," October 13, 2005, http://blogs.websidestory. com/datainsights/2005/09/firefox_cools_down_1.php, last accessed on November 26, 2007.

Coar, K. (2006) "The Open Source Definition (Annotated)." July 24, 2006, http://opensource.org/docs/definition.php. Last accessed on November 16, 2007.

CRN (2005) "Linux World Roundup: IBM Adds Firefox Support To Domino," August 9, 2005, http://www.crn.com/sections/breakingnews/dailyarchives. jhtml?articleId=168600040, last accessed on July 23, 2008.

Desmond, M, "IE 8: Compliance Fix or House of Cards?," January 24, 2008, http://reddevnews.com/blogs/weblog.aspx?blog=1852, last accessed January 28, 2008.

Domingo, J.S. Foxnews, "The laptop that could change the world," December 4, 2007. www.foxnews.com/story/0,2933,314802,00.html, last accessed December 5, 2007.

ETSI, (2007) "Mobile technologies GSM – Overview Standards". ETSI, Sophia-Antipolis, France, www.etsi.org/WebSite/Technologies/gsm.aspx last accessed December 03, 2007.

Foley, M.J., ZDNet, "What's next up for Internet Explorer? Microsoft opens up (a little)" May 01, 2007, http://blogs.zdnet.com/microsoft/?p=416, last accessed January 8, 2008.

Foley, M.J., ZDNet, October 25, 2007. "Up next: IE 8.0," http://blogs.zdnet. com/microsoft/?p=62, last accessed January 28, 2008.

FTP Backup Mosaic's licensing procedures, ftp://ftp.ncsa.uiuc.edu/Mosaic/ Licensing/, last accessed December 8, 2007.

Gaudin, S., Computerworld.com, "HP grabs punishing lead over Dell in PC market share," November 29, 2007, www.computerworld.com/action/ article.do?command=viewArticleBasicandtaxonomyName= laptopsandarticleId=9049999andtaxonomyId=76andintsrc=kc_top, last accessed December 08, 2007.

Google Annual Report 2006, www.propeller.com/viewstory/2007/03/02/ here-it-is-googles-annual-report-2006/?url=http%3A%2F%2Fwww.sec.gov %2FArchives%2Fedgar%2Fdata%2F1288776%2F000119312507044494%2 Fd10k.htmandframe=true, last accessed November 26, 2007.

Granneman, S. (2005) Don't click on the Blue E!, O'reilly.

Gromov, G.R. "History of Internet and WWW: the roads and crossroads of Internet history 1995–1998, http://netvalley.com/intvalold.html, last accessed December 08, 2007

Hamerly, J., Paquin, T., and Walton, S. (1999). Freeing the Source: the story of Mozilla, http://www.oreilly.com/catalog/opensources/book/netrev.html , last accessed on January 08, 2008.

Hecker, F. "Setting up shop: the business of open-source software," June 20, 2000, www.hecker.org/writings/setting-up-shop. last accessed on January 08, 2008.

Ives, B. and Jarvenpaa, S., Virtualschool.edu, 1994, What is the Internet and the world wide web?, http://virtualschool.edu/mon/CaseStudies/WebCase/ www.html, last accessed on December 08, 2007.

Infoworld.com, May 31, 2006. www.infoworld.com/article/06/05/31/78797_ HNballmerrandd_1.html?BUSINESS%20CHANGE%20MANAGEMENT, last accessed on November 26, 2007.

Keizer, G., "Linuxworld, Fix Firefox's memory problems, says Mozilla director," November 14, 2007, www.linuxworld.com.au/index.php/id; 2067098313;fp;4;fpid;4, last accessed on December 05, 2007

Knowledge@Wharton, "Will Firefox burn Internet Explorer," March 23, 2005, http://knowledge.wharton.upenn.edu/article.cfm?articleid=1162, last accessed on July 17, 2008.

Lawsky, D. "Microsoft finally bows to EU antitrust measures," October 22, 2007, http://investing.reuters.co.uk/news/articleinvesting.aspx?type= tnBusinessNewsandstoryID=2007-10-22T114840Z_01_BRE001179_ RTRIDST_0_BUSINESS-MICROSOFT-EU-DC.XML, last accessed on November 26, 2007.

Magid, L., Mercurynews.com, November 05, 2007, www.mercurynews.com/ business/ci_7374205?nclick_check=1, last accessed on December 05, 2007.

McFarlene, N. (2005) "Firefox hacks: tips and tools for next-generation web browsing," O'reilly.

Meyer, D., ZDAsia.com, www.zdnetasia.com/news/software/0,39044164, 62032062,00.htm, last accessed on November 26, 2007.

Microsoft Annual Report 2007, www.microsoft.com/msft, last accessed November 26, 2007.

Onestat.com Press Box (Onestat.com). (2002). April 29, 2002, www.onestat. com/html/aboutus_pressbox4.html, last accessed on December 15, 2007.

Perens, B. (1999) "It's time to talk about free software again," http://lists. debian.org/debian-devel/1999/02/msg01641.html, last accessed July 17, 2008.

Searchwindevelopment.com, http://searchwindevelopment.techtarget.com/ sDefinition/0,,sid8_gci211708,00.html, last accessed on November 16, 2007.

Shaver, M., and Ang, M., "Inside the lizard a look at the Mozilla technology and architecture," May 29, 2000, www.mozilla.org/docs/ora-oss2000/arch-overview/moz-arch-overview.pdf, last accessed on January 08, 2008.

Soghoian, C. (2007) "A dangerous conflict of interest between Firefox and Google," www.cnet.com/8301-13739_1-9776759-46.html?tag=blg.orig, last accessed on January 08, 2008.

Stallman, R. (1998) "It's still free software," February 16, 1998, http://lwn.net/1998/0219/a/rms.html, last accessed on November 15, 2007.

Wagner, J. (2005) "IBM Donates code to Firefox," August 15, 2005, www.internetnews.com/xSP/article.php/3527341, last accessed on November 16, 2007.

Xiti Browsers Barometer (Xitigroup.com). (2007). www.xitimonitor.com/en-us/browsers-barometer/index-1-2-3-0.html last accessed on December 08, 2007.

http://64.233.169.104/search?q=cache:Qdu1PNViy7IJ:www.websidestory.com/company/news-events/press-releases/view-release.html%3Fid%3D10
63%26year%3D2002+the+percentage+of+daily+internet+users+worldwide+that+access+the+internet+trough+a+particular+browseandhl=nlandct=cl
nkandcd=1, last accessed on December 08, 2007.

http://arstechnica.com/news.ars/post/20061010-7949.html, last accessed on December 15, 2007. (Cheng does not describe how the market shares were measured).

http://biztech.ericsink.com/Browser_Wars.html, last accessed on December 08, 2007. (For a firsthand account of the first browser war from the viewpoint of a Spyglass insider).

http://developer.mozilla.org/en/docs/Firefox_1.5_Beta_for_Developers, last accessed on November 16, 2007.

http://middleware.objectweb.org, last accessed on November 26, 2007.

http://moz.sillydog.org/archives/netscape_9_will_support_firefo.php, last accessed on November 26, 2007.

http://netscape.aol.com/, last accessed on February 12, 2008.

http://news.netcraft.com/, last accessed on December 08, 2007.

http://secunia.com/product/11/, last accessed on July 17, 2008.

http://secunia.com/product/4227/, last accessed on July 17, 2008.

http://steelgryphon.com/blog/?p=39, last accessed on November 16, 2007.

http://steelgryphon.com/blog/index.php?p=34, last accessed on November 16, 2007.

http://steelgryphon.com/blog/index.php?p=37, last accessed on November 16, 2007.

http://weblogs.mozillazine.org/asa/archives/2005/11/more_than_two_m.html, last accessed on November 16, 2007.

http://weblogs.mozillazine.org/mitchell/archives/2005/01/ben_and_mozilla_1.html, last accessed on November 16, 2007.

www.apple.com/safari, last accessed on December 17, 2007.

www.betanews.com/article/Mozillas_Firefox_usage_estimates_climb_by_15_M_since_July/1196713676, last accessed on December 08, 2007.

www.blooberry.com/indexdot/history/ie.htm, last accessed on November 16, 2007.

www.catb.org/%7Eesr/writings/cathedral-bazaar/cathedral-bazaar/ar01s13.html, last accessed on July 17, 2008.

www.census.gov, last accessed on November 16, 2007.

www.cnn.com/TECH/computing/9810/08/browser.idg/, last accessed on December 08, 2007.

www.crn.com/sections/breakingnews/dailyarchives.jhtml?articleId=168600040, last accessed on November 16, 2007.

www.defendingthefox.com, last accessed on January 08, 2008.

www.e-janco.com/browser.htm, last accessed on December 15, 2007.

www.google.com/search?hl=enandq=link%3Awww.mozilla.org%2Fproducts%2Ffirefox%2FandbtnG=Search, last accessed on January 08, 2008.

www.google.com/search?q=link%3Awww.mozilla.organdbtnG=Google+Search, last accessed on January 08, 2008.

www.holgermetzger.de/Netscape_History.html, last accessed on July 17, 2008.

www.microsoft.com/resources/sharedsource/Articles/MicrosoftandOpenSource.mspx. Microsoft and Open Source, last accessed on July 17, 2008.

www.microsoft.com/resources/sharedsource/Initiative/FAQ.mspx, FAQ Shared Source Initiative, last accessed on July 17, 2008.

www.microsoft.com/resources/sharedsource/Licensing/default.mspx, last accessed on January 10, 2008.

www.microsoft.com/windowsserversystem/facts/default.mspx, last accessed on November 26, 2007.

www.microsoft-watch.com/article2/0,2180,1765128,00.asp, last accessed on July 17, 2008.

www.mozilla.org/about/staff, last accessed on January 08, 2008.

www.mozilla.org/free-faq.html, last accessed on December 08, 2007.

www.mozilla.org/press/mozilla-2005-02-16.html, last accessed on December 08, 2007. www.mozilla.org/press/mozilla-2005-10-19.html, last accessed on December 08, 2007.

www.mozilla.org/products/choosing-products.html, last accessed on December 08, 2007.

www.mozilla.org/projects/seamonkey/, last accessed on December 08, 2007.

www.mozilla.org/seamonkey-transition.html, last accessed on December 08, 2007).

www.mozilla.org/university/HOF.html, last accessed on January 08, 2008.

www.ncsa.uiuc.edu, last accessed on January 08, 2008.

www.news.com/8301-13580_3-9773836-39.html, last accessed on January 08, 2008.

www.nu.nl/news/1354239/52/Opnieuw_mededingingsklacht_tegen_Microsoft.html, last accessed on December 13, 2007.

www.onestat.com, last accessed on December 02, 2007.

www.onestat.com/html/aboutus_pressbox23.html, last accessed on December 15, 2007.

www.onestat.com/html/aboutus_pressbox44-mozilla-firefox-has-slightly-increased.html, last accessed on December 15, 2007.

www.onestat.com/html/aboutus_pressbox49-microsoft-internet-explorer-7-usage.html, last accessed on December 15, 2007.

www.onestat.com/html/aboutus_pressbox53-firefox-mozilla-browser-market-share.html, last accessed on December 02, 2007.

www.quickonlinetips.com/archives/2006/08/mozilla-firefox-browser-crosses-200-million-downloads/, last accessed on January 08, 2008.

www.quickonlinetips.com/archives/2007/02/mozilla-firefox-tops-300-million-downloads/, last accessed on January 08, 2008.

www.quirksmode.org/browsers, last accessed on July 17, 2008.

www.slate.com/id/2103152/, last accessed on November 16, 2007.

www.softwaremag.com, last accessed on December 11, 2007.

www.sourceforge.net, last accessed on December 08, 2007.

www.techworld.com/applications/news/index.cfm?NewsID=5604, March 21, 2006, last accessed on November 26, 2007.

www.techworld.com/networking/news/index.cfm?NewsID=5115, last accessed on July 17, 2008.

www.theinquirer.net/?article=28380, last accessed on July 17, 2008.

www.w3.org, last accessed on November 16, 2007.

www.w3.org/Style/CSS/Disclosures, last accessed on November 16, 2007.

www.w3.org/TR/REC-DOM-Level-1, last accessed on July 17, 2008.

www.websidestory.com, last accessed on December 08, 2007.

www.wired.com/news/antitrust/0,1551,35212,00.html. April 11, 2002.

www-306.ibm.com/able/news/firefox.html, last accessed on July 17, 2008.

Index